THE X-RAY PICTURE BOOK *of* INCREDIBLE CREATURES

Author:
Gerald Legg holds
a doctorate in zoology from
Manchester University. He worked
in West Africa for several years as
lecturer and rain forest researcher. Dr
Legg's current position is biologist at
the Booth Museum of Natural
History in Brighton; he also wrote
Amazing Animals, another book in
this series.

Creator:
David Salariya was born in
Dundee, Scotland, where he studied
illustration and printmaking,
concentrating on book design in his
post-graduate year. He has illustrated
a wide range of books on botanical,
historical and mythical subjects. He
has designed and created the
Timelines, *New View* and *X-ray Picture
Book* series for Watts. He lives in
Brighton with his wife, the
illustrator Shirley Willis.

David Salariya   *Series Editor*
Penny Clarke   *Book Editor*

Illustrator:
Carolyn Scrace is a graduate of
Brighton College of Art, specialising
in illustration. She has worked in
animation, advertising and
children's non-fiction, and enjoys
natural history illustration. She is a
major contributor to *The X-ray
Picture Book* series, in particular
Amazing Animals, *Your Body* and
Dinosaurs.

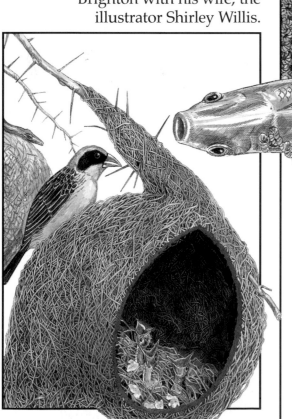

First published in 1995 by
Watts Books, London
This edition published in 1995
exclusively for Parrallel Books,
Units 13-17, Avonbridge Trading
Estate, Atlantic Road,
Avonmouth,
Bristol, BS11 9QD

ISBN 0 7496 1718 7

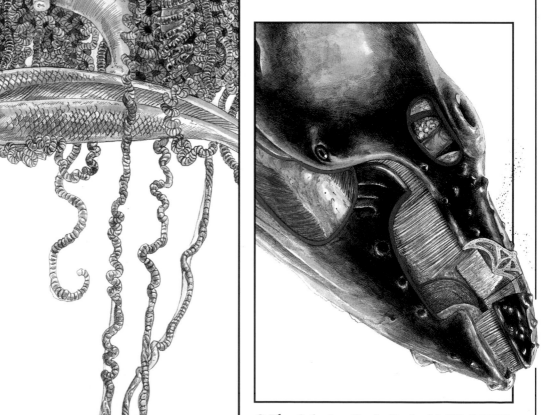

Printed in Belgium

A CIP catalogue record for this book is available
from the British Library.

The X-RAY PICTURE BOOK of INCREDIBLE CREATURES

Written by
GERALD LEGG

Illustrated by
CAROLYN SCRACE

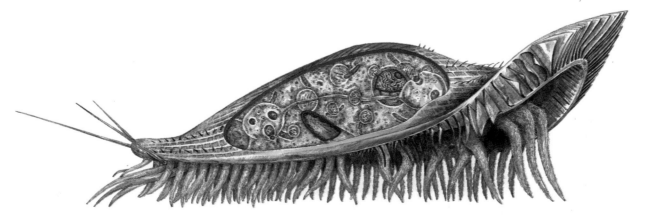

·PARRALLEL·

CONTENTS

DINOSAURS

MICROSCOPIC MARVELS

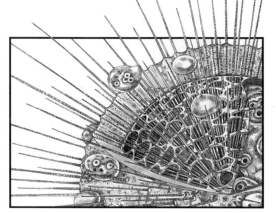

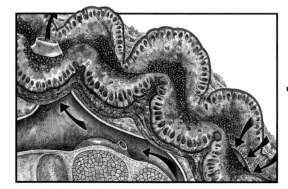

INVERTEBRATES

LIVING IN WATER

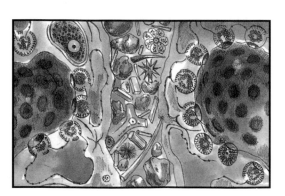

ANIMAL ARCHITECTS

INCREDIBLE WAYS

26

TO SURVIVE, ANIMALS must find food, avoid being eaten and reproduce. During the milions of years there has been life on Earth, some incredible ways of survival have evolved.

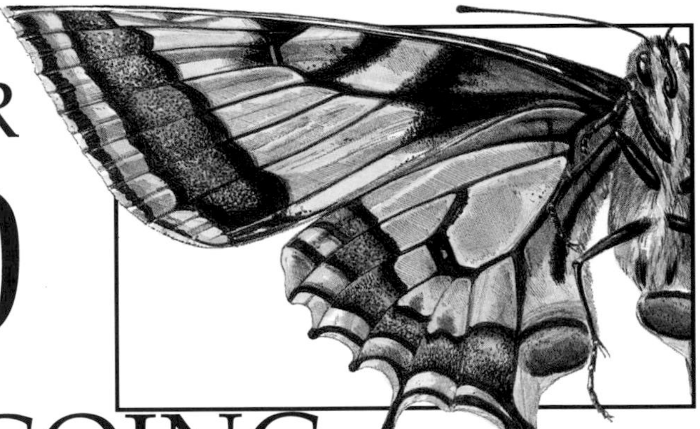

UP IN THE AIR

30

CREATURES THAT FLY have many advantages. They can escape predators, find food, look for a mate and find somewhere better to live. Insects and birds dominate the air.

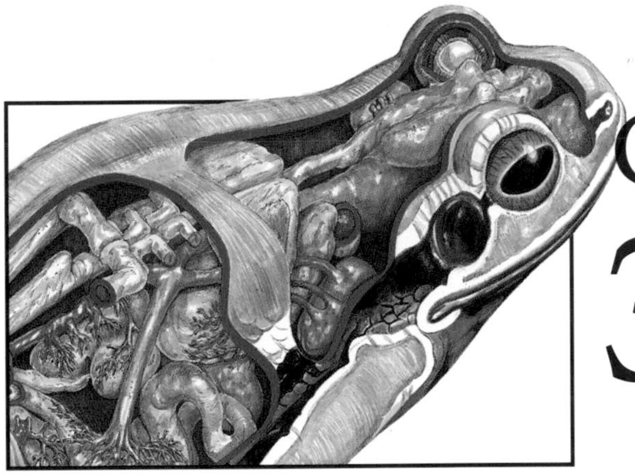

GOING, GOING . . .

34

NO SPECIES OF PLANT or animal exists for ever. Most species die out quite naturally, to be replaced by better-adapted species. People have upset this balance.

GONE FOR EVER

38

FOSSILS PROVIDE MOST evidence of the creatures that once lived on Earth. But not all extinct creatures are ancient. Some were killed off by people a few centuries ago.

MYTHICAL MONSTERS

42

FROM ALL OVER THE WORLD, from all times and cultures, come tales of mythical monsters. Aliens and UFOs are just modern relations of dragons and mermaids!

46 GLOSSARY

48 INDEX

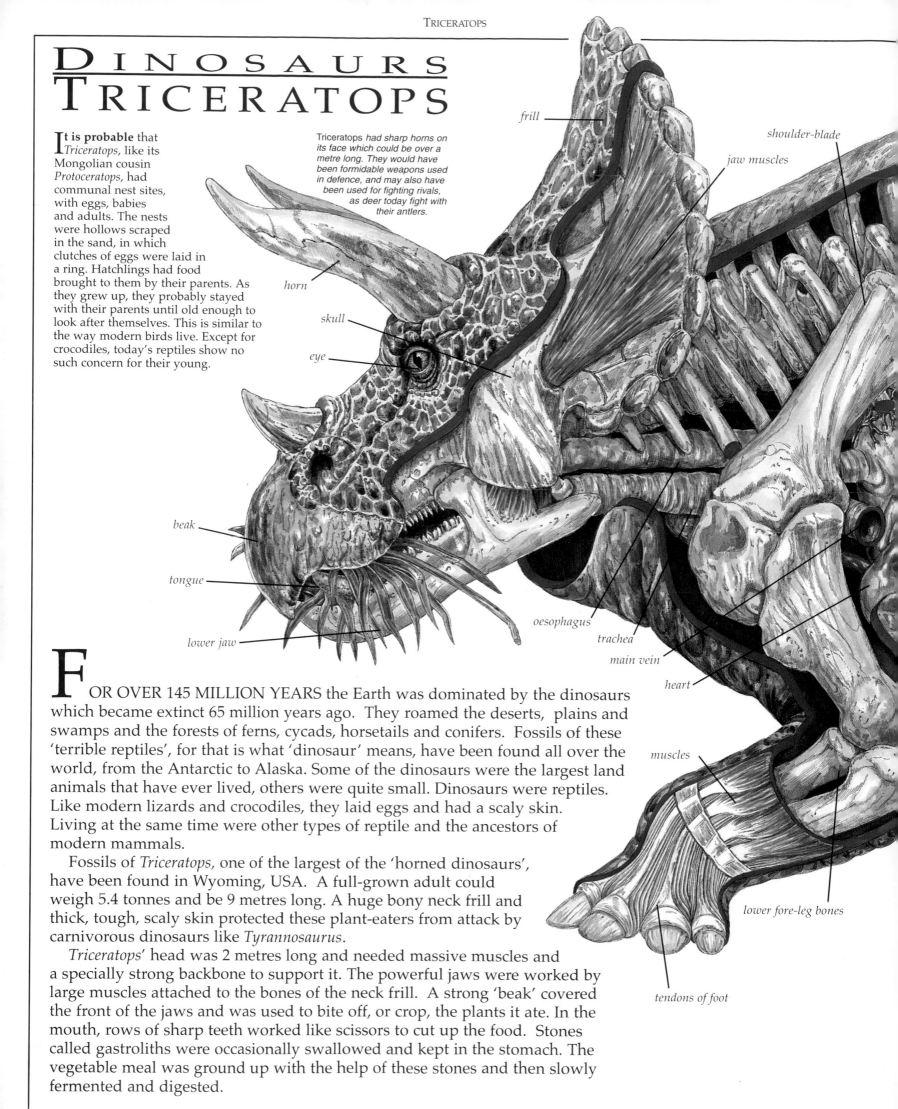

DINOSAURS
TRICERATOPS

It is probable that *Triceratops*, like its Mongolian cousin *Protoceratops*, had communal nest sites, with eggs, babies and adults. The nests were hollows scraped in the sand, in which clutches of eggs were laid in a ring. Hatchlings had food brought to them by their parents. As they grew up, they probably stayed with their parents until old enough to look after themselves. This is similar to the way modern birds live. Except for crocodiles, today's reptiles show no such concern for their young.

Triceratops had sharp horns on its face which could be over a metre long. They would have been formidable weapons used in defence, and may also have been used for fighting rivals, as deer today fight with their antlers.

frill

shoulder-blade

jaw muscles

horn

skull

eye

beak

tongue

lower jaw

oesophagus

trachea

main vein

heart

muscles

lower fore-leg bones

tendons of foot

FOR OVER 145 MILLION YEARS the Earth was dominated by the dinosaurs which became extinct 65 million years ago. They roamed the deserts, plains and swamps and the forests of ferns, cycads, horsetails and conifers. Fossils of these 'terrible reptiles', for that is what 'dinosaur' means, have been found all over the world, from the Antarctic to Alaska. Some of the dinosaurs were the largest land animals that have ever lived, others were quite small. Dinosaurs were reptiles. Like modern lizards and crocodiles, they laid eggs and had a scaly skin. Living at the same time were other types of reptile and the ancestors of modern mammals.

Fossils of *Triceratops,* one of the largest of the 'horned dinosaurs', have been found in Wyoming, USA. A full-grown adult could weigh 5.4 tonnes and be 9 metres long. A huge bony neck frill and thick, tough, scaly skin protected these plant-eaters from attack by carnivorous dinosaurs like *Tyrannosaurus.*

Triceratops' head was 2 metres long and needed massive muscles and a specially strong backbone to support it. The powerful jaws were worked by large muscles attached to the bones of the neck frill. A strong 'beak' covered the front of the jaws and was used to bite off, or crop, the plants it ate. In the mouth, rows of sharp teeth worked like scissors to cut up the food. Stones called gastroliths were occasionally swallowed and kept in the stomach. The vegetable meal was ground up with the help of these stones and then slowly fermented and digested.

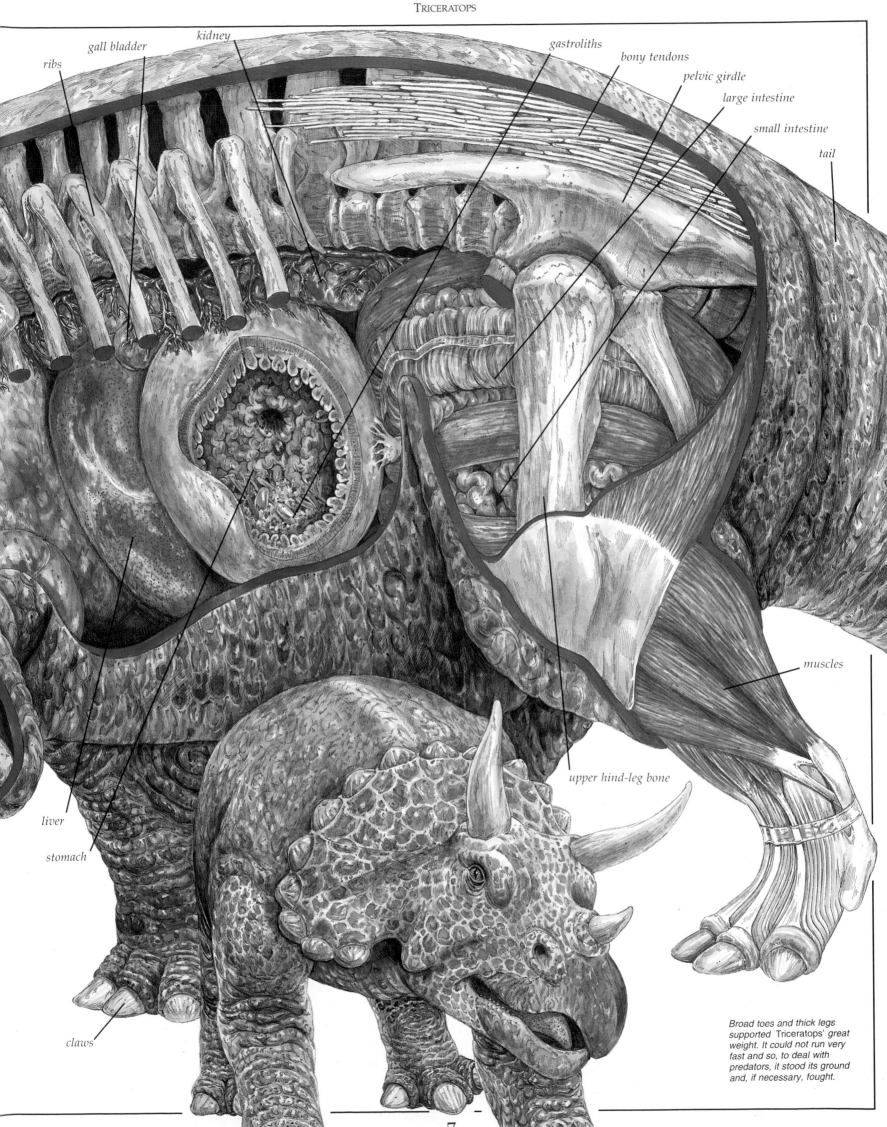

ribs

gall bladder

kidney

gastroliths

bony tendons

pelvic girdle

large intestine

small intestine

tail

muscles

upper hind-leg bone

liver

stomach

claws

Broad toes and thick legs
supported Triceratops' great
weight. It could not run very
fast and so, to deal with
predators, it stood its ground
and, if necessary, fought.

Brachiosaurus *needed a long neck to reach the ground to drink, but why its nostrils were so high on its head nobody knows.* nostril

At a quick glance, some dinosaurs look like huge versions of modern lizards. But dinosaurs were built quite differently from lizards. Lizards have short legs that stick out on either side of their bodies. This means they move inefficiently: waddling along and having to raise themselves off the ground. When resting, a lizard flops on its stomach and chest. Dinosaurs, on the other hand, had long legs tucked under their bodies. This enabled them to move efficiently and keep their bodies clear of the ground.

bony crest

Brachiosaurus, 22.5m, 150-128 million years ago
Weighing over 75 tonnes, these giants were plant-eaters. They had long necks and front legs: Brachiosaurus means 'arm reptile'. Like the long front legs of a giraffe, those of Brachiosaurus helped it reach high into the trees for food. It may also have been able to rear up on its hind legs to reach even higher.

long neck to reach tall vegetation

thick, strong legs to support massive body

arm bones support large wings

D I N O S A U R S
A SUCCESS STORY

DINOSAURS WERE EXTREMELY SUCCESSFUL and can be compared with the mammals of today, living in a wide variety of different habitats and in different ways. Some had dagger-like teeth and fed on flesh. Others had scissor-like teeth for cutting up plants. There are several reasons why dinosaurs were so successful. Dry, desert conditions, favourable for reptiles, were widespread when dinosaurs were most numerous. Many of the animals that competed with the dinosaurs became rarer at this time. Dinosaurs' brains were more complex, so they would have been more intelligent and adaptable. Finally, the bones of many dinosaurs had a similar structure to warm-blooded mammals, which makes some scientists believe that dinosaurs were warm-blooded. If so, the warm-blooded dinosaurs could be more active than cold-blooded reptiles.

Why did dinosaurs become extinct? Mammals and other dinosaurs eating their eggs could not have been the cause. Fossils show that mass extinctions occurred 64 million years ago. Perhaps a giant meteorite crashed into the Earth, throwing up dust and blocking out the sun. A star may have exploded, bathing the Earth in fatal cosmic rays. Gradual changes in the Earth's climate may also have caused their death. We will never know for certain why dinosaurs died out. But perhaps they didn't, and are still here, represented by the birds.

Pteranodon, 7m wing-span, 85-65 million years ago
Living at the same time as the dinosaurs was a large flying reptile, Pteranodon. It had broad wings, which enabled it to glide long distances. Its long toothless beak, with which it caught fish, was counterbalanced by a bony crest.

Stegoceras, 20m, 84-68 million years ago
Stegoceras, the 'thick-headed reptile', gets its name from the thick, horny, domed covering on its head. Fossils show that some of these herbivores had larger domed heads than others, which suggests that there were differences between males and females.

Tyrannosaurus, 14m,
70-64 million years ago
Tyrannosaurus, or 'tyrant reptile', was the
world's largest land-living meat-eater. It
was a scavenger, attracted to the smell of
decaying carcasses.

None of the dinosaurs could fly, and none
lived in the sea, but flying reptiles, like the
pterosaurs, and marine reptiles, like the
ichthyosaurs and *plesiosaurs*, lived at the same
time. Crocodiles evolved from ancestors of the
dinosaurs and lived alongside them, but, unlike
their distant dinosaur cousins, they did not
become extinct.

hollow crest

strong teeth
and jaws for
tearing flesh

tail to act
as balance

Parasaurolophus, 10m,
80-64 million years ago
Parasaurolophus *means*
'beside ridged reptile' which
refers to the two ridges on
either side of the striking,
metre-long crest of hollow
bone on its head. Crests
could help individuals
recognise each other, act as
sound resonators (like the
beak of a hornbill) and
provide an acute sense of
smell.

front feet with
4 toes

thick, horny
protective
head covering

hind feet with
3 toes

front feet
with sharp
claws

double row of
defensive
spines

sickle-like claw

Velociraptor, 1.8m,
77-70 million years ago
Velociraptor, or 'speedy
predator', had a sickle-like claw
on its hind foot which could
disembowel its prey. Fossils of
Velociraptor and Protoceratops *in*
mortal combat have been found in
Mongolia.

Kentrosaurus, 2.5m,
150-140 million years ago
Kentrosaurus, or 'prickly
reptile', was a slow-moving
plant-eater and needed the
double row of spines down
its back and tail for defence.

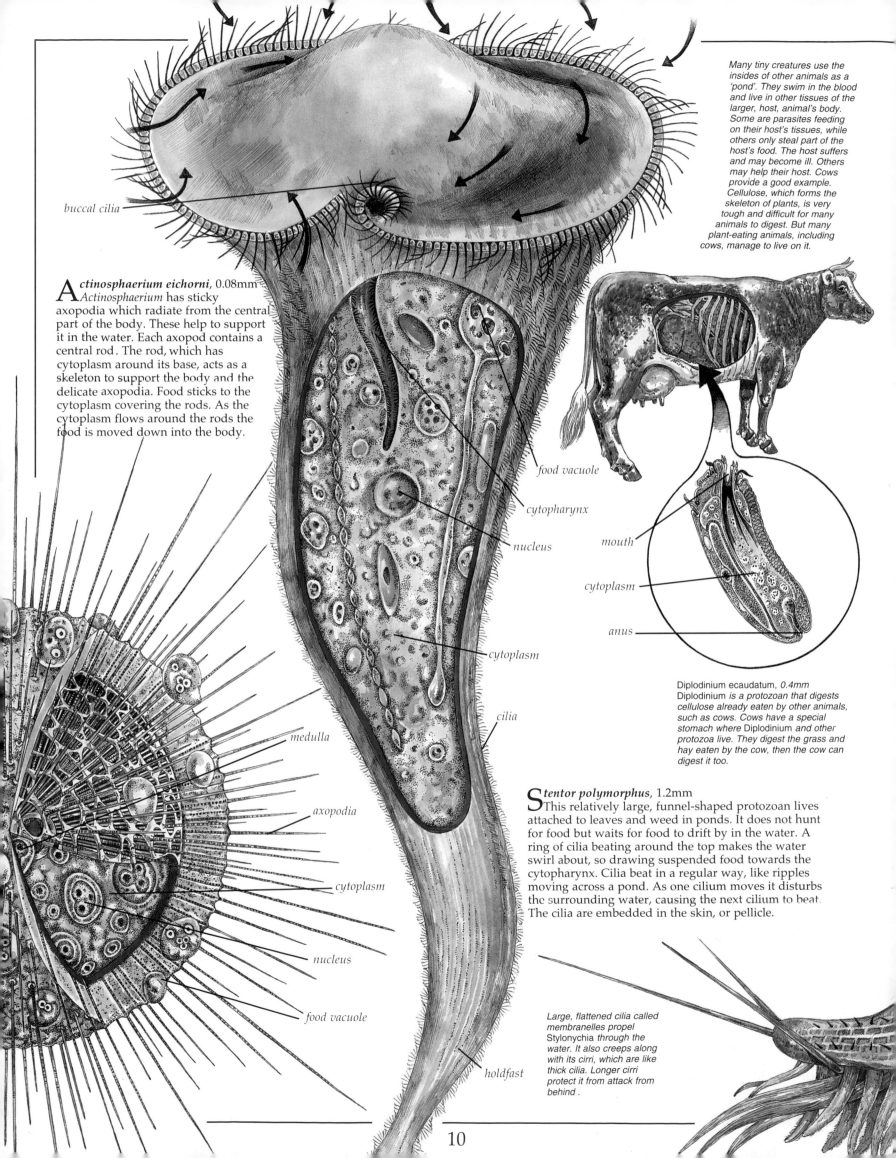

buccal cilia

Many tiny creatures use the insides of other animals as a 'pond'. They swim in the blood and live in other tissues of the larger, host, animal's body. Some are parasites feeding on their host's tissues, while others only steal part of the host's food. The host suffers and may become ill. Others may help their host. Cows provide a good example. Cellulose, which forms the skeleton of plants, is very tough and difficult for many animals to digest. But many plant-eating animals, including cows, manage to live on it.

Actinosphaerium eichorni, 0.08mm
Actinosphaerium has sticky axopodia which radiate from the central part of the body. These help to support it in the water. Each axopod contains a central rod. The rod, which has cytoplasm around its base, acts as a skeleton to support the body and the delicate axopodia. Food sticks to the cytoplasm covering the rods. As the cytoplasm flows around the rods the food is moved down into the body.

food vacuole

cytopharynx

nucleus

cytoplasm

mouth

cytoplasm

anus

Diplodinium ecaudatum, *0.4mm*
Diplodinium is a protozoan that digests cellulose already eaten by other animals, such as cows. Cows have a special stomach where Diplodinium and other protozoa live. They digest the grass and hay eaten by the cow, then the cow can digest it too.

cilia

medulla

axopodia

cytoplasm

nucleus

food vacuole

Stentor polymorphus, 1.2mm
This relatively large, funnel-shaped protozoan lives attached to leaves and weed in ponds. It does not hunt for food but waits for food to drift by in the water. A ring of cilia beating around the top makes the water swirl about, so drawing suspended food towards the cytopharynx. Cilia beat in a regular way, like ripples moving across a pond. As one cilium moves it disturbs the surrounding water, causing the next cilium to beat. The cilia are embedded in the skin, or pellicle.

Large, flattened cilia called membranelles propel Stylonychia *through the water. It also creeps along with its cirri, which are like thick cilia. Longer cirri protect it from attack from behind .*

holdfast

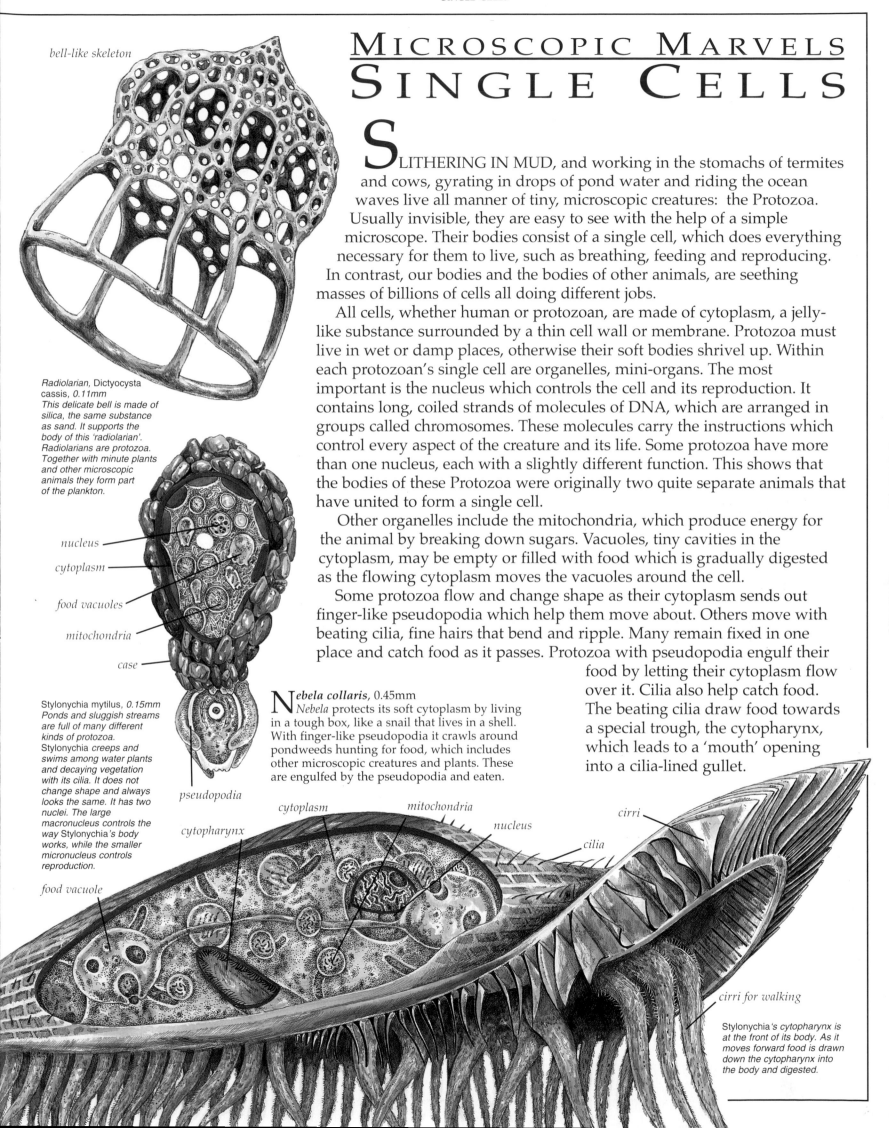

bell-like skeleton

MICROSCOPIC MARVELS
SINGLE CELLS

SLITHERING IN MUD, and working in the stomachs of termites and cows, gyrating in drops of pond water and riding the ocean waves live all manner of tiny, microscopic creatures: the Protozoa. Usually invisible, they are easy to see with the help of a simple microscope. Their bodies consist of a single cell, which does everything necessary for them to live, such as breathing, feeding and reproducing. In contrast, our bodies and the bodies of other animals, are seething masses of billions of cells all doing different jobs.

All cells, whether human or protozoan, are made of cytoplasm, a jelly-like substance surrounded by a thin cell wall or membrane. Protozoa must live in wet or damp places, otherwise their soft bodies shrivel up. Within each protozoan's single cell are organelles, mini-organs. The most important is the nucleus which controls the cell and its reproduction. It contains long, coiled strands of molecules of DNA, which are arranged in groups called chromosomes. These molecules carry the instructions which control every aspect of the creature and its life. Some protozoa have more than one nucleus, each with a slightly different function. This shows that the bodies of these Protozoa were originally two quite separate animals that have united to form a single cell.

Other organelles include the mitochondria, which produce energy for the animal by breaking down sugars. Vacuoles, tiny cavities in the cytoplasm, may be empty or filled with food which is gradually digested as the flowing cytoplasm moves the vacuoles around the cell.

Some protozoa flow and change shape as their cytoplasm sends out finger-like pseudopodia which help them move about. Others move with beating cilia, fine hairs that bend and ripple. Many remain fixed in one place and catch food as it passes. Protozoa with pseudopodia engulf their food by letting their cytoplasm flow over it. Cilia also help catch food. The beating cilia draw food towards a special trough, the cytopharynx, which leads to a 'mouth' opening into a cilia-lined gullet.

Radiolarian, Dictyocysta cassis, 0.11mm
This delicate bell is made of silica, the same substance as sand. It supports the body of this 'radiolarian'. Radiolarians are protozoa. Together with minute plants and other microscopic animals they form part of the plankton.

nucleus

cytoplasm

food vacuoles

mitochondria

case

Stylonychia mytilus, 0.15mm
Ponds and sluggish streams are full of many different kinds of protozoa. Stylonychia *creeps and swims among water plants and decaying vegetation with its cilia. It does not change shape and always looks the same. It has two nuclei. The large macronucleus controls the way Stylonychia's body works, while the smaller micronucleus controls reproduction.*

food vacuole

pseudopodia

N*ebela collaris*, 0.45mm
Nebela protects its soft cytoplasm by living in a tough box, like a snail that lives in a shell. With finger-like pseudopodia it crawls around pondweeds hunting for food, which includes other microscopic creatures and plants. These are engulfed by the pseudopodia and eaten.

cytoplasm

cytopharynx

mitochondria

nucleus

cirri

cilia

cirri for walking

Stylonychia's *cytopharynx is at the front of its body. As it moves forward food is drawn down the cytopharynx into the body and digested.*

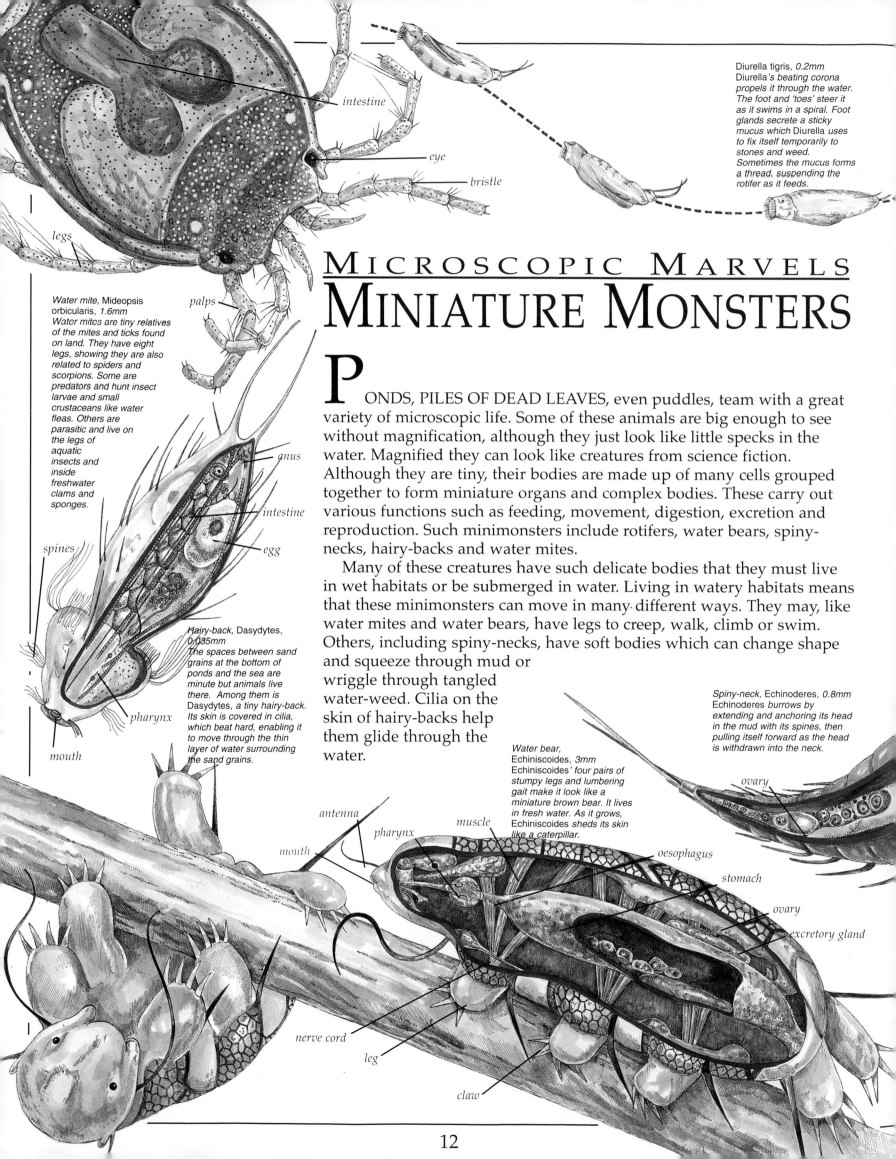

intestine

eye

bristle

legs

palps

Diurella tigris, 0.2mm
Diurella's beating corona propels it through the water. The foot and 'toes' steer it as it swims in a spiral. Foot glands secrete a sticky mucus which Diurella uses to fix itself temporarily to stones and weed. Sometimes the mucus forms a thread, suspending the rotifer as it feeds.

Water mite, Mideopsis orbicularis, 1.6mm
Water mites are tiny relatives of the mites and ticks found on land. They have eight legs, showing they are also related to spiders and scorpions. Some are predators and hunt insect larvae and small crustaceans like water fleas. Others are parasitic and live on the legs of aquatic insects and inside freshwater clams and sponges.

anus

intestine

egg

spines

pharynx

mouth

Hairy-back, Dasydytes, 0.035mm
The spaces between sand grains at the bottom of ponds and the sea are minute but animals live there. Among them is Dasydytes, a tiny hairy-back. Its skin is covered in cilia, which beat hard, enabling it to move through the thin layer of water surrounding the sand grains.

MICROSCOPIC MARVELS
MINIATURE MONSTERS

P ONDS, PILES OF DEAD LEAVES, even puddles, team with a great variety of microscopic life. Some of these animals are big enough to see without magnification, although they just look like little specks in the water. Magnified they can look like creatures from science fiction. Although they are tiny, their bodies are made up of many cells grouped together to form miniature organs and complex bodies. These carry out various functions such as feeding, movement, digestion, excretion and reproduction. Such minimonsters include rotifers, water bears, spiny-necks, hairy-backs and water mites.

Many of these creatures have such delicate bodies that they must live in wet habitats or be submerged in water. Living in watery habitats means that these minimonsters can move in many different ways. They may, like water mites and water bears, have legs to creep, walk, climb or swim. Others, including spiny-necks, have soft bodies which can change shape and squeeze through mud or wriggle through tangled water-weed. Cilia on the skin of hairy-backs help them glide through the water.

Spiny-neck, Echinoderes, 0.8mm
Echinoderes burrows by extending and anchoring its head in the mud with its spines, then pulling itself forward as the head is withdrawn into the neck.

ovary

Water bear, Echiniscoides, 3mm
Echiniscoides' four pairs of stumpy legs and lumbering gait make it look like a miniature brown bear. It lives in fresh water. As it grows, Echiniscoides sheds its skin like a caterpillar.

antenna

mouth

pharynx

muscle

oesophagus

stomach

ovary

excretory gland

nerve cord

leg

claw

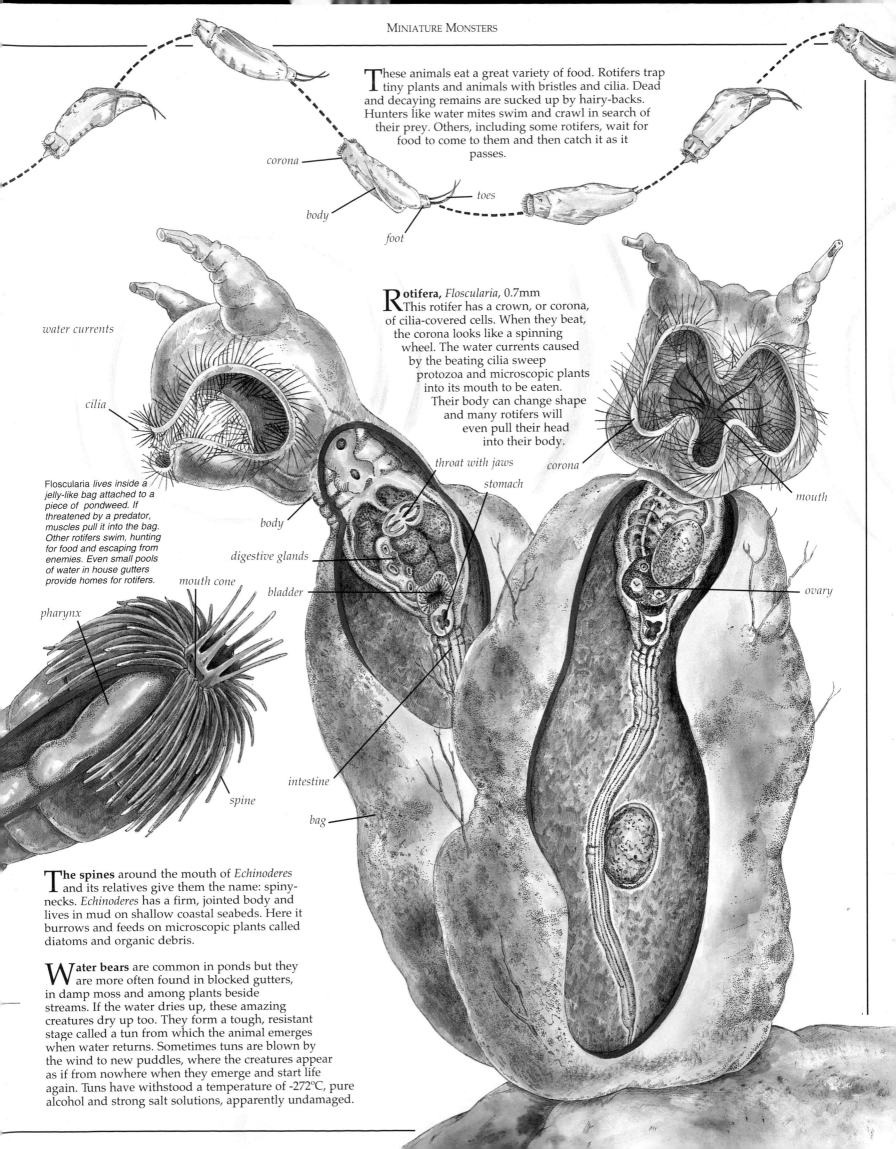

These animals eat a great variety of food. Rotifers trap tiny plants and animals with bristles and cilia. Dead and decaying remains are sucked up by hairy-backs. Hunters like water mites swim and crawl in search of their prey. Others, including some rotifers, wait for food to come to them and then catch it as it passes.

corona

body

toes

foot

water currents

cilia

Floscularia lives inside a jelly-like bag attached to a piece of pondweed. If threatened by a predator, muscles pull it into the bag. Other rotifers swim, hunting for food and escaping from enemies. Even small pools of water in house gutters provide homes for rotifers.

mouth cone

pharynx

spine

Rotifera, *Floscularia*, 0.7mm
This rotifer has a crown, or corona, of cilia-covered cells. When they beat, the corona looks like a spinning wheel. The water currents caused by the beating cilia sweep protozoa and microscopic plants into its mouth to be eaten. Their body can change shape and many rotifers will even pull their head into their body.

throat with jaws

stomach

corona

mouth

body

digestive glands

bladder

ovary

intestine

bag

The spines around the mouth of *Echinoderes* and its relatives give them the name: spiny-necks. *Echinoderes* has a firm, jointed body and lives in mud on shallow coastal seabeds. Here it burrows and feeds on microscopic plants called diatoms and organic debris.

Water bears are common in ponds but they are more often found in blocked gutters, in damp moss and among plants beside streams. If the water dries up, these amazing creatures dry up too. They form a tough, resistant stage called a tun from which the animal emerges when water returns. Sometimes tuns are blown by the wind to new puddles, where the creatures appear as if from nowhere when they emerge and start life again. Tuns have withstood a temperature of -272°C, pure alcohol and strong salt solutions, apparently undamaged.

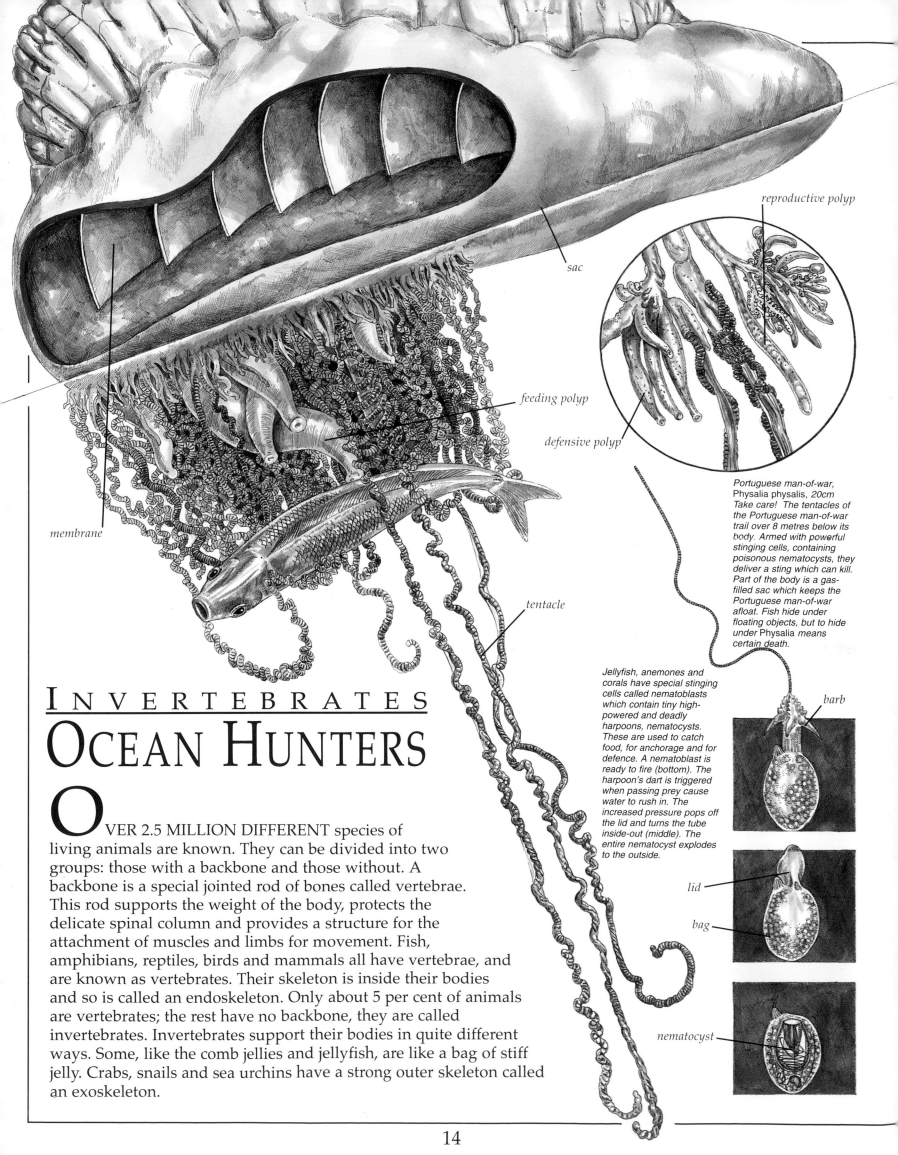

sac

reproductive polyp

feeding polyp

defensive polyp

membrane

tentacle

Portuguese man-of-war, Physalia physalis, 20cm Take care! The tentacles of the Portuguese man-of-war trail over 8 metres below its body. Armed with powerful stinging cells, containing poisonous nematocysts, they deliver a sting which can kill. Part of the body is a gas-filled sac which keeps the Portuguese man-of-war afloat. Fish hide under floating objects, but to hide under Physalia means certain death.

Jellyfish, anemones and corals have special stinging cells called nematoblasts which contain tiny high-powered and deadly harpoons, nematocysts. These are used to catch food, for anchorage and for defence. A nematoblast is ready to fire (bottom). The harpoon's dart is triggered when passing prey cause water to rush in. The increased pressure pops off the lid and turns the tube inside-out (middle). The entire nematocyst explodes to the outside.

barb

lid

bag

nematocyst

INVERTEBRATES
OCEAN HUNTERS

OVER 2.5 MILLION DIFFERENT species of living animals are known. They can be divided into two groups: those with a backbone and those without. A backbone is a special jointed rod of bones called vertebrae. This rod supports the weight of the body, protects the delicate spinal column and provides a structure for the attachment of muscles and limbs for movement. Fish, amphibians, reptiles, birds and mammals all have vertebrae, and are known as vertebrates. Their skeleton is inside their bodies and so is called an endoskeleton. Only about 5 per cent of animals are vertebrates; the rest have no backbone, they are called invertebrates. Invertebrates support their bodies in quite different ways. Some, like the comb jellies and jellyfish, are like a bag of stiff jelly. Crabs, snails and sea urchins have a strong outer skeleton called an exoskeleton.

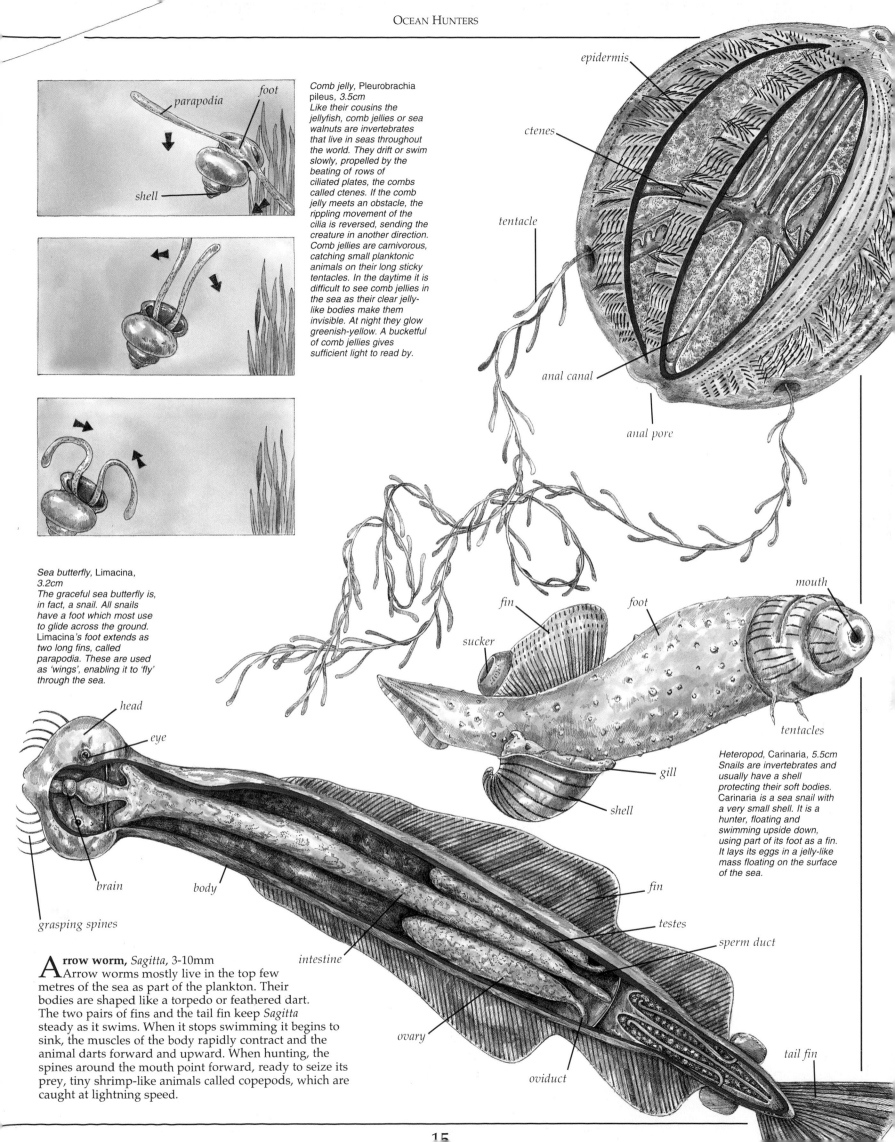

parapodia *foot*

shell

Comb jelly, Pleurobrachia pileus, 3.5cm
Like their cousins the jellyfish, comb jellies or sea walnuts are invertebrates that live in seas throughout the world. They drift or swim slowly, propelled by the beating of rows of ciliated plates, the combs called ctenes. If the comb jelly meets an obstacle, the rippling movement of the cilia is reversed, sending the creature in another direction. Comb jellies are carnivorous, catching small planktonic animals on their long sticky tentacles. In the daytime it is difficult to see comb jellies in the sea as their clear jelly-like bodies make them invisible. At night they glow greenish-yellow. A bucketful of comb jellies gives sufficient light to read by.

epidermis

ctenes

tentacle

anal canal

anal pore

Sea butterfly, Limacina, 3.2cm
The graceful sea butterfly is, in fact, a snail. All snails have a foot which most use to glide across the ground. Limacina's foot extends as two long fins, called parapodia. These are used as 'wings', enabling it to 'fly' through the sea.

mouth

fin *foot*

sucker

tentacles

gill

shell

Heteropod, Carinaria, 5.5cm
Snails are invertebrates and usually have a shell protecting their soft bodies. Carinaria is a sea snail with a very small shell. It is a hunter, floating and swimming upside down, using part of its foot as a fin. It lays its eggs in a jelly-like mass floating on the surface of the sea.

head

eye

brain *body*

grasping spines

intestine

fin

testes

sperm duct

ovary

oviduct

tail fin

Arrow worm, *Sagitta*, 3-10mm
Arrow worms mostly live in the top few metres of the sea as part of the plankton. Their bodies are shaped like a torpedo or feathered dart. The two pairs of fins and the tail fin keep *Sagitta* steady as it swims. When it stops swimming it begins to sink, the muscles of the body rapidly contract and the animal darts forward and upward. When hunting, the spines around the mouth point forward, ready to seize its prey, tiny shrimp-like animals called copepods, which are caught at lightning speed.

Horseshoe crab, Limulus polyphemus, 60cm
Horseshoe crabs are members of the large group of invertebrates called arthropods, which means 'armoured limb'. Like spiders and scorpions, they have a single pair of pincer-like jaws, called chelicerae.

Horseshoe crabs eat worms, shellfish and seaweed. They pick up food with their pincer-like limbs and grind it up with the spiny 'elbows', or gnathobases, of their legs. The small particles of food are then picked up by the chelicerae and put into the mouth.

gnathobase

chelicera

carapace

gill flaps

outlet siphon

digestive gland

mouth

intake siphon

mantle

shell

gills

INVERTEBRATES
ON THE SEABED

MANY ADULT INVERTEBRATES are sedentary – they remain in one place for most of their lives. Instead of searching for food they wait for food to come to them. Some, like clams, filter food from the water. Siphons suck in water and pump it through gills covered in mucus. These filter off particles that are then carried to the mouth by beating cilia. Sea mats and some worms have tentacles which are also covered in cilia and mucus. They wave these in the water to catch food.

Most sedentary invertebrates live in protective cases. Clams have two hinged shells made of a chalky material. If frightened, they close the shells to protect their soft bodies. Sea mats retreat into cases made of chitin, a material similar to that of our fingernails.

Sedentary invertebrates are not always immobile. In order to spread and find new places to live many species have swimming planktonic larvae. Larvae look quite different from their parents. As they grow, the larvae gradually change to look like their parents. This process is called metamorphosis. Horseshoe crabs, prawns, starfish and sea urchins are not sedentary; they can move about looking for food or a mate, but they, too, have swimming planktonic larvae. As adults they have tough exoskeletons to protect their soft bodies, just like shrimps and insects. Special jointed jaws bite, crush and grind food. Sea urchins have jaws with five long, curved teeth to nibble food off rocks. Their exoskeletons are chalky and covered in sharp spines to deter predators.

Giant clam, Tridacna gigas, 1.1m
The giant clam breathes through gills – large flat sheets of tissue – protected by the two big shells. Many veins take blood to the gills to pick up oxygen from the water for breathing and to lose waste carbon dioxide. This is the largest mollusc with a shell (the giant squid is the largest mollusc) and is found in the Indian and Pacific oceans. If a diver puts a foot between the open shells, powerful muscles quickly contract, closing the shells and trapping the diver's foot.

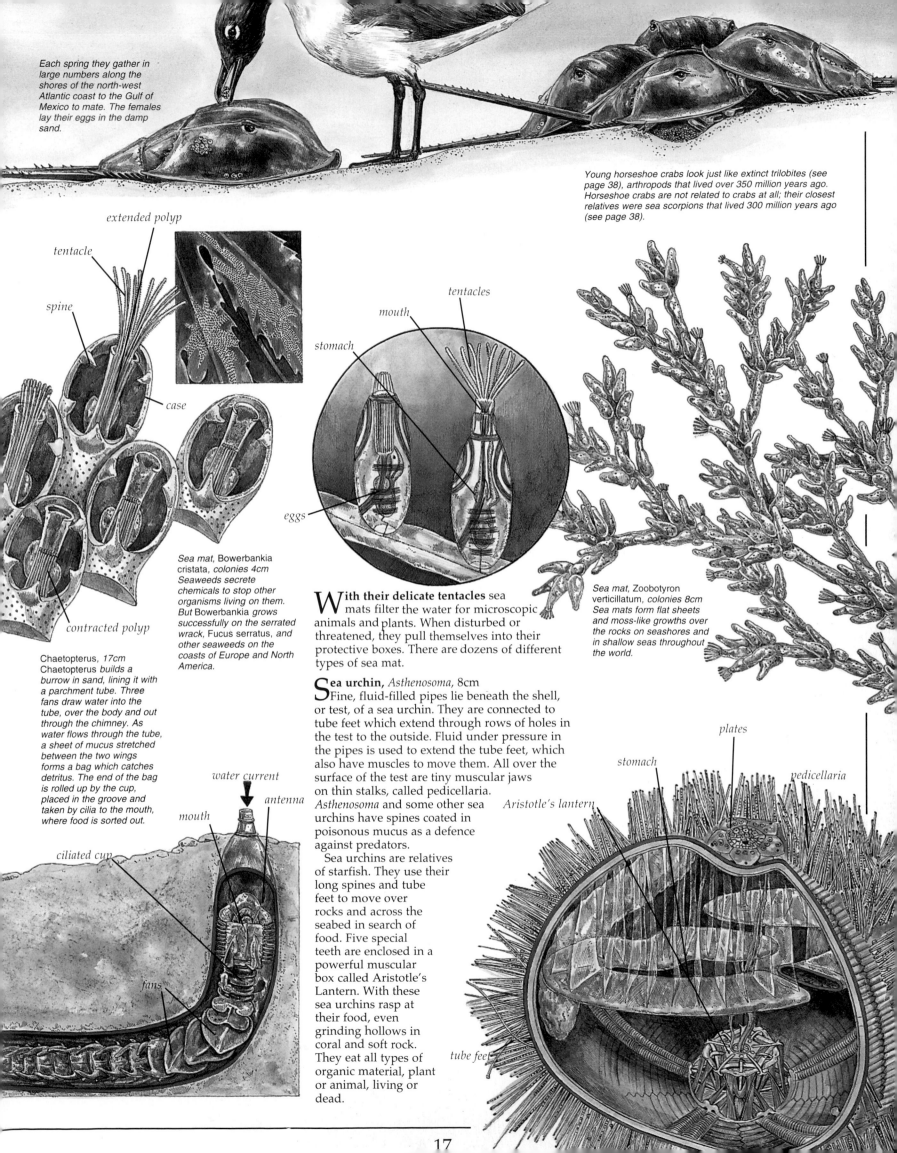

Each spring they gather in large numbers along the shores of the north-west Atlantic coast to the Gulf of Mexico to mate. The females lay their eggs in the damp sand.

Young horseshoe crabs look just like extinct trilobites (see page 38), arthropods that lived over 350 million years ago. Horseshoe crabs are not related to crabs at all; their closest relatives were sea scorpions that lived 300 million years ago (see page 38).

extended polyp

tentacle

spine

case

contracted polyp

Chaetopterus, *17cm*
Chaetopterus builds a burrow in sand, lining it with a parchment tube. Three fans draw water into the tube, over the body and out through the chimney. As water flows through the tube, a sheet of mucus stretched between the two wings forms a bag which catches detritus. The end of the bag is rolled up by the cup, placed in the groove and taken by cilia to the mouth, where food is sorted out.

Sea mat, Bowerbankia cristata, colonies 4cm Seaweeds secrete chemicals to stop other organisms living on them. But Bowerbankia grows successfully on the serrated wrack, Fucus serratus, and other seaweeds on the coasts of Europe and North America.

tentacles

mouth

stomach

eggs

water current

antenna

mouth

ciliated cup

fans

With their delicate tentacles sea mats filter the water for microscopic animals and plants. When disturbed or threatened, they pull themselves into their protective boxes. There are dozens of different types of sea mat.

Sea urchin, *Asthenosoma*, 8cm
Fine, fluid-filled pipes lie beneath the shell, or test, of a sea urchin. They are connected to tube feet which extend through rows of holes in the test to the outside. Fluid under pressure in the pipes is used to extend the tube feet, which also have muscles to move them. All over the surface of the test are tiny muscular jaws on thin stalks, called pedicellaria. *Asthenosoma* and some other sea urchins have spines coated in poisonous mucus as a defence against predators.
   Sea urchins are relatives of starfish. They use their long spines and tube feet to move over rocks and across the seabed in search of food. Five special teeth are enclosed in a powerful muscular box called Aristotle's Lantern. With these sea urchins rasp at their food, even grinding hollows in coral and soft rock. They eat all types of organic material, plant or animal, living or dead.

Sea mat, Zoobotyron verticillatum, colonies 8cm Sea mats form flat sheets and moss-like growths over the rocks on seashores and in shallow seas throughout the world.

plates

stomach

pedicellaria

Aristotle's lantern

tube feet

intestine

stomach

crop

liver

oesophagus

flipper ('wing')

Galapagos marine iguana, Amblyrhynchus cristatus, 1.4m
Marine iguanas are the only sea lizards living today, although they bask and breed on land. In the water their broad tails make them excellent swimmers. Unlike most reptiles, marine iguanas are herbivores, eating seaweed with their rounded teeth.

Emperor penguin, Aptenodytes forsteri, 1.12m
Penguins are flightless birds. On land they appear clumsy, waddling around on stumpy legs. Underwater, however, they 'fly', propelled by their powerful webbed feet and stubby wings, chasing fish which they catch in their strong beaks.

artery

vein

trachea

heart

skin

LIVING IN WATER
VERTEBRATES

MILLIONS OF YEARS AGO the oceans were the birthplace of life on planet Earth. To live out of water needed special adaptations. These included a skeleton to support the body against gravity; organs to breathe air; a waterproof skin to stop the body drying out; a method of excreting waste that uses little or no water; a method of reproduction that prevents eggs and sperm drying up. It was not until about 400 million years ago that creatures solved most of these problems and were able to invade the land. Many different types of animal evolved and became better adapted to life on land than in water. However, the descendants of some of these vertebrates, including reptiles, birds and mammals, went back to living in water, at least for part of their lives. Many aquatic vertebrates, like crocodiles, alligators, penguins and walruses, can live on dry land as well as in water. They need water for feeding and as somewhere to escape from enemies. They need the land for breeding and rearing their young. Others spend their whole lives in water. Whales, dolphins, sea snakes and manatees never go onto land, except accidentally. They still have legs, useless on land but, as fins or flippers, ideally adapted to steering through water.

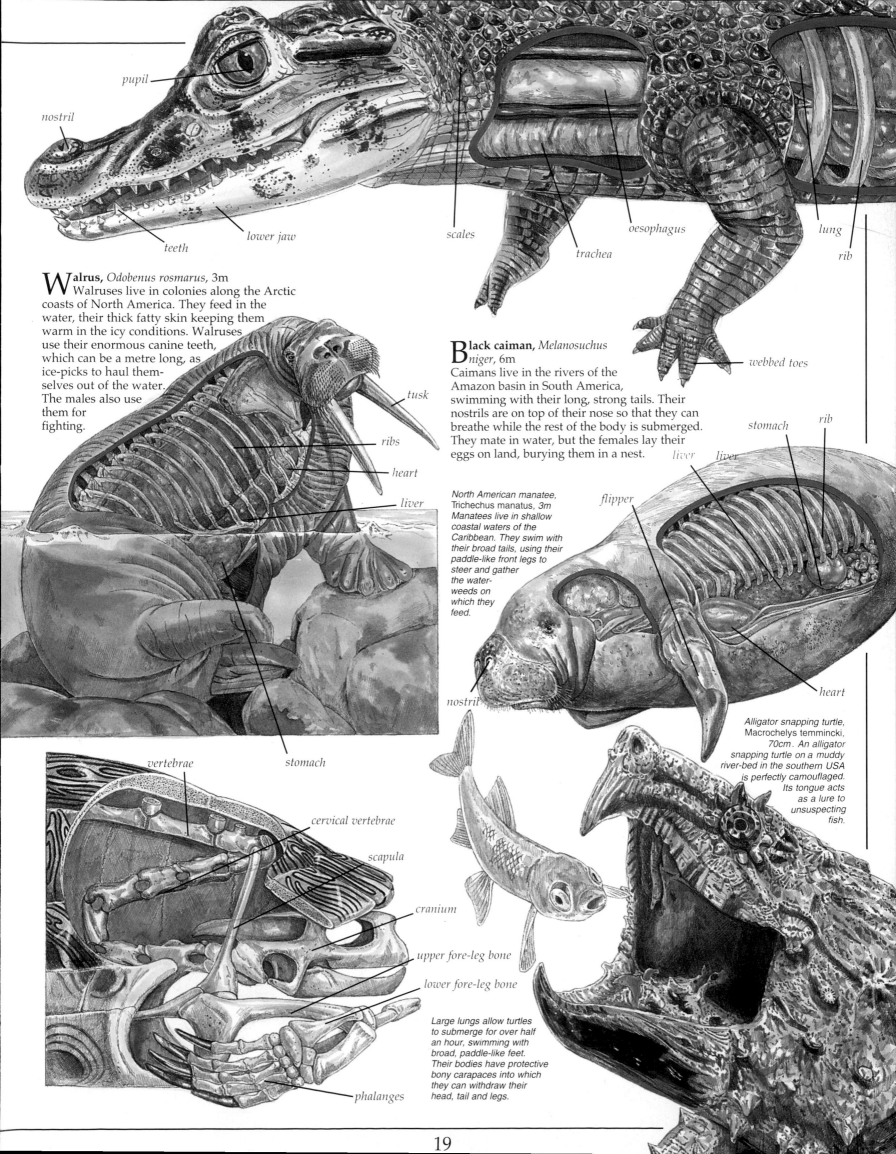

pupil

nostril

teeth

lower jaw

scales

trachea

oesophagus

lung

rib

webbed toes

Walrus, *Odobenus rosmarus*, 3m
Walruses live in colonies along the Arctic
coasts of North America. They feed in the
water, their thick fatty skin keeping them
warm in the icy conditions. Walruses
use their enormous canine teeth,
which can be a metre long, as
ice-picks to haul them-
selves out of the water.
The males also use
them for
fighting.

tusk

ribs

heart

liver

Black caiman, *Melanosuchus
niger*, 6m
Caimans live in the rivers of the
Amazon basin in South America,
swimming with their long, strong tails. Their
nostrils are on top of their nose so that they can
breathe while the rest of the body is submerged.
They mate in water, but the females lay their
eggs on land, burying them in a nest.

stomach

rib

liver

liver

North American manatee,
Trichechus manatus, *3m*
Manatees live in shallow
coastal waters of the
Caribbean. They swim with
their broad tails, using their
paddle-like front legs to
steer and gather
the water-
weeds on
which they
feed.

flipper

nostril

heart

vertebrae

stomach

cervical vertebrae

scapula

cranium

upper fore-leg bone

lower fore-leg bone

Alligator snapping turtle,
Macrochelys temmincki,
70cm. An alligator
snapping turtle on a muddy
river-bed in the southern USA
is perfectly camouflaged.
Its tongue acts
as a lure to
unsuspecting
fish.

Large lungs allow turtles
to submerge for over half
an hour, swimming with
broad, paddle-like feet.
Their bodies have protective
bony carapaces into which
they can withdraw their
head, tail and legs.

phalanges

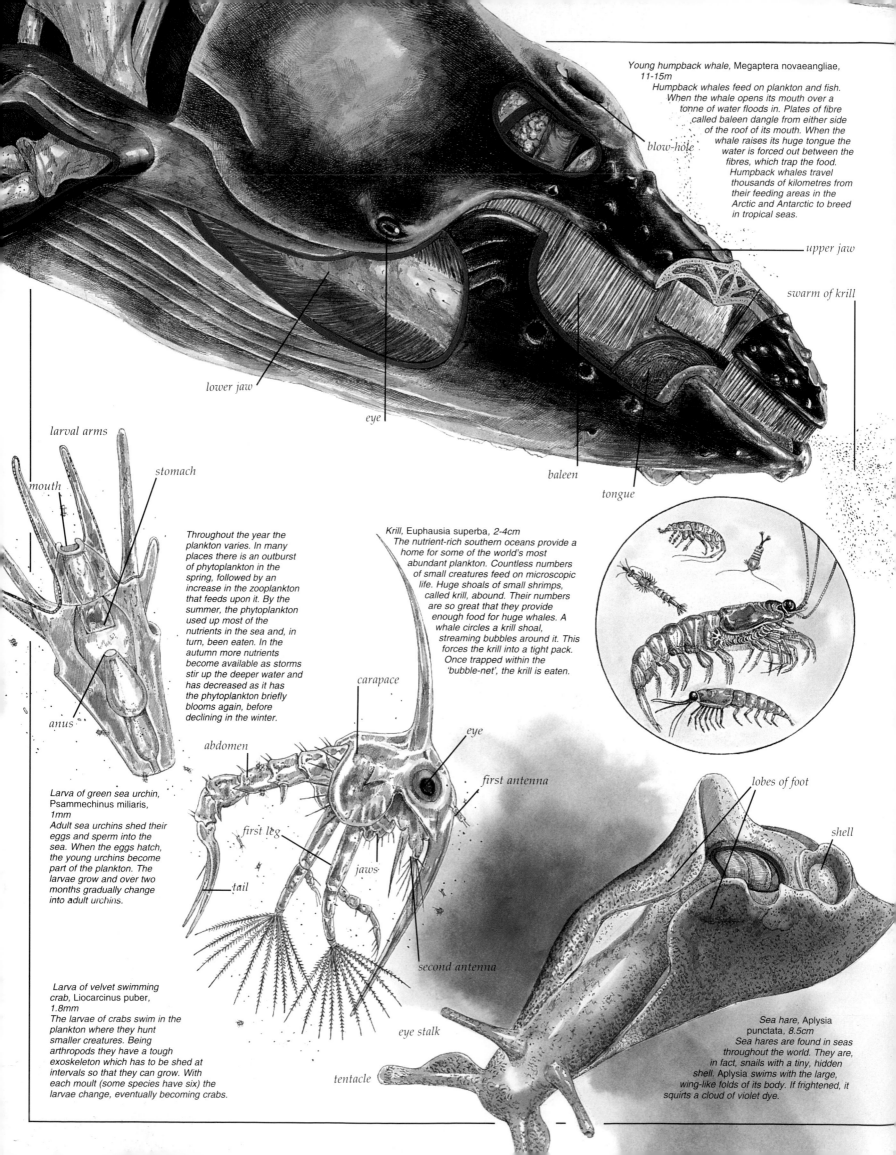

Young humpback whale, Megaptera novaeangliae, 11-15m
Humpback whales feed on plankton and fish. When the whale opens its mouth over a tonne of water floods in. Plates of fibre called baleen dangle from either side of the roof of its mouth. When the whale raises its huge tongue the water is forced out between the fibres, which trap the food. Humpback whales travel thousands of kilometres from their feeding areas in the Arctic and Antarctic to breed in tropical seas.

blow-hole

upper jaw

swarm of krill

lower jaw

eye

baleen

tongue

larval arms

stomach

mouth

anus

Throughout the year the plankton varies. In many places there is an outburst of phytoplankton in the spring, followed by an increase in the zooplankton that feeds upon it. By the summer, the phytoplankton used up most of the nutrients in the sea and, in turn, been eaten. In the autumn more nutrients become available as storms stir up the deeper water and has decreased as it has the phytoplankton briefly blooms again, before declining in the winter.

Krill, Euphausia superba, 2-4cm
The nutrient-rich southern oceans provide a home for some of the world's most abundant plankton. Countless numbers of small creatures feed on microscopic life. Huge shoals of small shrimps, called krill, abound. Their numbers are so great that they provide enough food for huge whales. A whale circles a krill shoal, streaming bubbles around it. This forces the krill into a tight pack. Once trapped within the 'bubble-net', the krill is eaten.

Larva of green sea urchin, Psammechinus miliaris, 1mm
Adult sea urchins shed their eggs and sperm into the sea. When the eggs hatch, the young urchins become part of the plankton. The larvae grow and over two months gradually change into adult urchins.

carapace

eye

abdomen

first antenna

first leg

jaws

tail

second antenna

lobes of foot

shell

eye stalk

Larva of velvet swimming crab, Liocarcinus puber, 1.8mm
The larvae of crabs swim in the plankton where they hunt smaller creatures. Being arthropods they have a tough exoskeleton which has to be shed at intervals so that they can grow. With each moult (some species have six) the larvae change, eventually becoming crabs.

tentacle

Sea hare, Aplysia punctata, 8.5cm
Sea hares are found in seas throughout the world. They are, in fact, snails with a tiny, hidden shell. Aplysia swims with the large, wing-like folds of its body. If frightened, it squirts a cloud of violet dye.

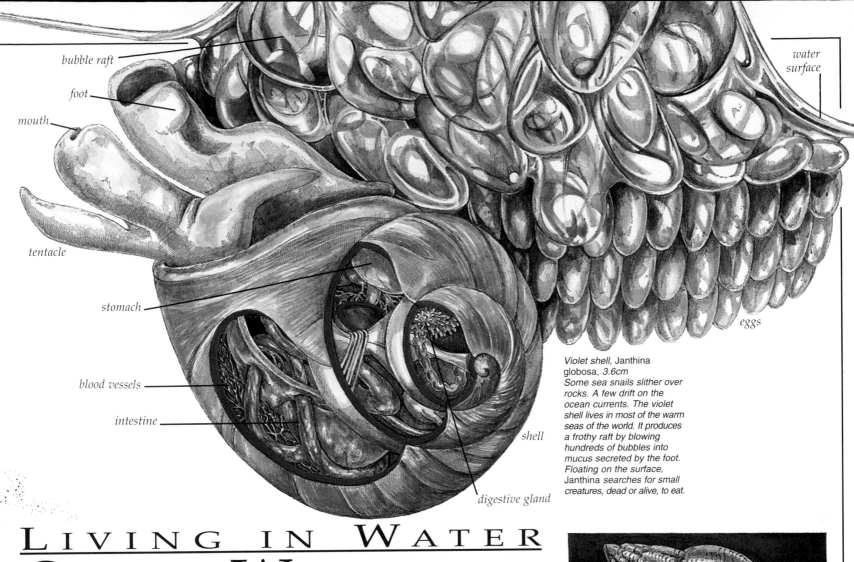

bubble raft
foot
mouth
tentacle
stomach
blood vessels
intestine
shell
digestive gland

water surface
eggs

Violet shell, Janthina globosa, 3.6cm
Some sea snails slither over rocks. A few drift on the ocean currents. The violet shell lives in most of the warm seas of the world. It produces a frothy raft by blowing hundreds of bubbles into mucus secreted by the foot. Floating on the surface, Janthina searches for small creatures, dead or alive, to eat.

LIVING IN WATER
OCEAN WANDERERS

THE TOP THREE OR FOUR METRES of the world's seas are home to countless tiny plants and animals. This is the world of the plankton, a community living and drifting freely in the water. The plants are called phytoplankton and the animals zooplankton. The phytoplankton use sunlight, water and carbon dioxide to grow. During the day they stay near the surface to be in the sunlight; at night they sink a little. The zooplankton, which can only swim short distances, follow this 'vertical migration'. Many creatures, including ourselves, depend on these plants which produce over half of the oxygen we need to breathe. The tiny plants are eaten by small animals which in turn are eaten by larger ones and so on. Giant whales, the world's largest living creatures, depend on plankton for their food. Some animals, like the violet shell and krill, spend their entire lives as part of the plankton. For others, including dog-winkles and sea urchins, it is just one stage of their life cycle.

Plankton may drift vast distances, circulating on the ocean currents. The seas of the world have different temperatures, salts and nutrients. These differences affect the type of plankton present. Cold and temperate seas, like those of Antarctica and the North Atlantic, are very rich in nutrients and support huge communities of plankton. Tropical seas like the central Pacific have very little plankton. There is often more plankton near coasts than in mid-ocean, because of the presence of nutrients washed off the land.

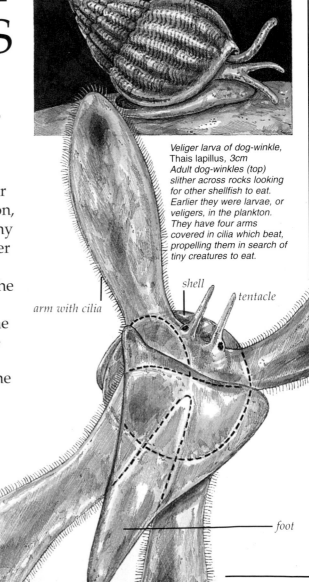

Veliger larva of dog-winkle, Thais lapillus, 3cm
Adult dog-winkles (top) slither across rocks looking for other shellfish to eat. Earlier they were larvae, or veligers, in the plankton. They have four arms covered in cilia which beat, propelling them in search of tiny creatures to eat.

arm with cilia
shell
tentacle
foot

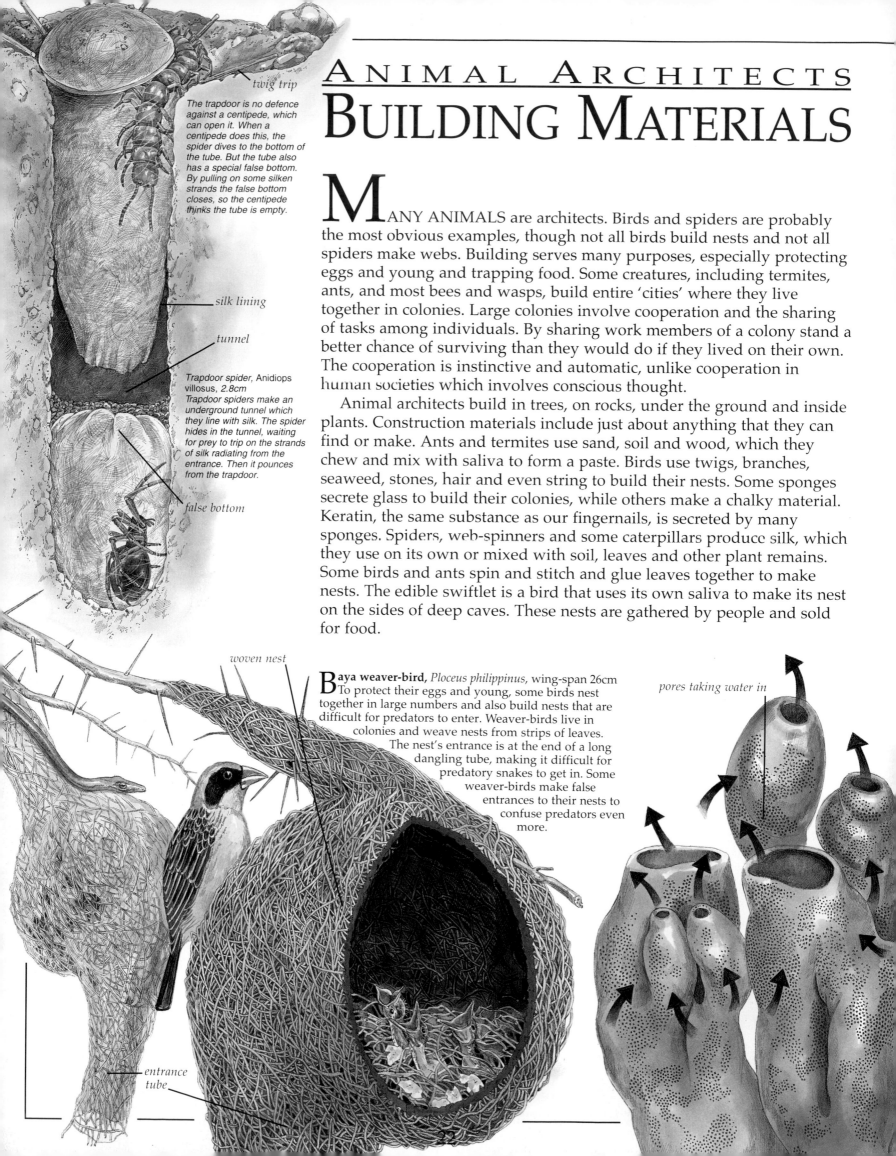

The trapdoor is no defence against a centipede, which can open it. When a centipede does this, the spider dives to the bottom of the tube. But the tube also has a special false bottom. By pulling on some silken strands the false bottom closes, so the centipede thinks the tube is empty.

twig trip

silk lining

tunnel

Trapdoor spider, Anidiops villosus, 2.8cm
Trapdoor spiders make an underground tunnel which they line with silk. The spider hides in the tunnel, waiting for prey to trip on the strands of silk radiating from the entrance. Then it pounces from the trapdoor.

false bottom

BUILDING MATERIALS

MANY ANIMALS are architects. Birds and spiders are probably the most obvious examples, though not all birds build nests and not all spiders make webs. Building serves many purposes, especially protecting eggs and young and trapping food. Some creatures, including termites, ants, and most bees and wasps, build entire 'cities' where they live together in colonies. Large colonies involve cooperation and the sharing of tasks among individuals. By sharing work members of a colony stand a better chance of surviving than they would do if they lived on their own. The cooperation is instinctive and automatic, unlike cooperation in human societies which involves conscious thought.

Animal architects build in trees, on rocks, under the ground and inside plants. Construction materials include just about anything that they can find or make. Ants and termites use sand, soil and wood, which they chew and mix with saliva to form a paste. Birds use twigs, branches, seaweed, stones, hair and even string to build their nests. Some sponges secrete glass to build their colonies, while others make a chalky material. Keratin, the same substance as our fingernails, is secreted by many sponges. Spiders, web-spinners and some caterpillars produce silk, which they use on its own or mixed with soil, leaves and other plant remains. Some birds and ants spin and stitch and glue leaves together to make nests. The edible swiftlet is a bird that uses its own saliva to make its nest on the sides of deep caves. These nests are gathered by people and sold for food.

woven nest

Baya weaver-bird, *Ploceus philippinus*, wing-span 26cm
To protect their eggs and young, some birds nest together in large numbers and also build nests that are difficult for predators to enter. Weaver-birds live in colonies and weave nests from strips of leaves. The nest's entrance is at the end of a long dangling tube, making it difficult for predatory snakes to get in. Some weaver-birds make false entrances to their nests to confuse predators even more.

pores taking water in

entrance tube

Orb-web spider building web
If insects evolved wings to escape from predatory spiders, they were not safe for long. Spiders spin strong silken webs to trap their airborne prey.

Fantastic webs are built by the orb-web spiders. Some of these can be over two metres across and catch small birds. Most spiders spin a new web each morning before daybreak.

The first strands act as a scaffold for the spider to work from. The spider often has to walk and drop some distance before it can bridge the gaps between the supports.

The scaffold enables the spider to make the spokes of its web. Starting at the hub, it lays down a spiral of dry silk. This acts as a guide for the spider to lay down special sticky silk.

Harlequin tusk-fish, Lienardella fasciatus

Sponge, *Druinella purpurea*, 20cm
Sponges have internal skeletons (endo-skeletons). Different species of sponge use different building materials, including glass and calcium carbonate, a chalk-like substance. These materials are embedded in the sponges' soft body tissue – like reinforcing steel rods in concrete. A sponge's walls are perforated by tiny holes which are the openings of cavities. These cavities are connected by tubes which, in turn, connect with to larger tubes that eventually join the central cavity. Beating flagellae in the cavities draw water into the sponge. Food is filtered out and the water ejected through the osculum.

Sea whip, *Mopsella ellisi*, 1m
Sea whips have skeletons of horny keratin. Each whip is, in fact, a colony of thousands of individuals sharing food and building the colony's skeleton in the warm tropical seas of the Indian and Pacific oceans.

Moorish idol, Zanchus cornutus

sponge skeletons

osculum

spicule *central cavity*

Soft coral, Dendronephthya species

Hydrocoral, Distichopora violacea

Stony coral, Favia bowerbanki, *polyps 1-3mm*
Stony corals have skeletons of chalky calcium carbonate. Individual coral animals, or polyps, may be small, but colonies can become large enough to form reefs. The Great Barrier Reef of Australia, where *Favia* lives, is the world's largest non-man-made structure.

tentacles

skeleton

membrane

Clown fish, Amphiprion percula

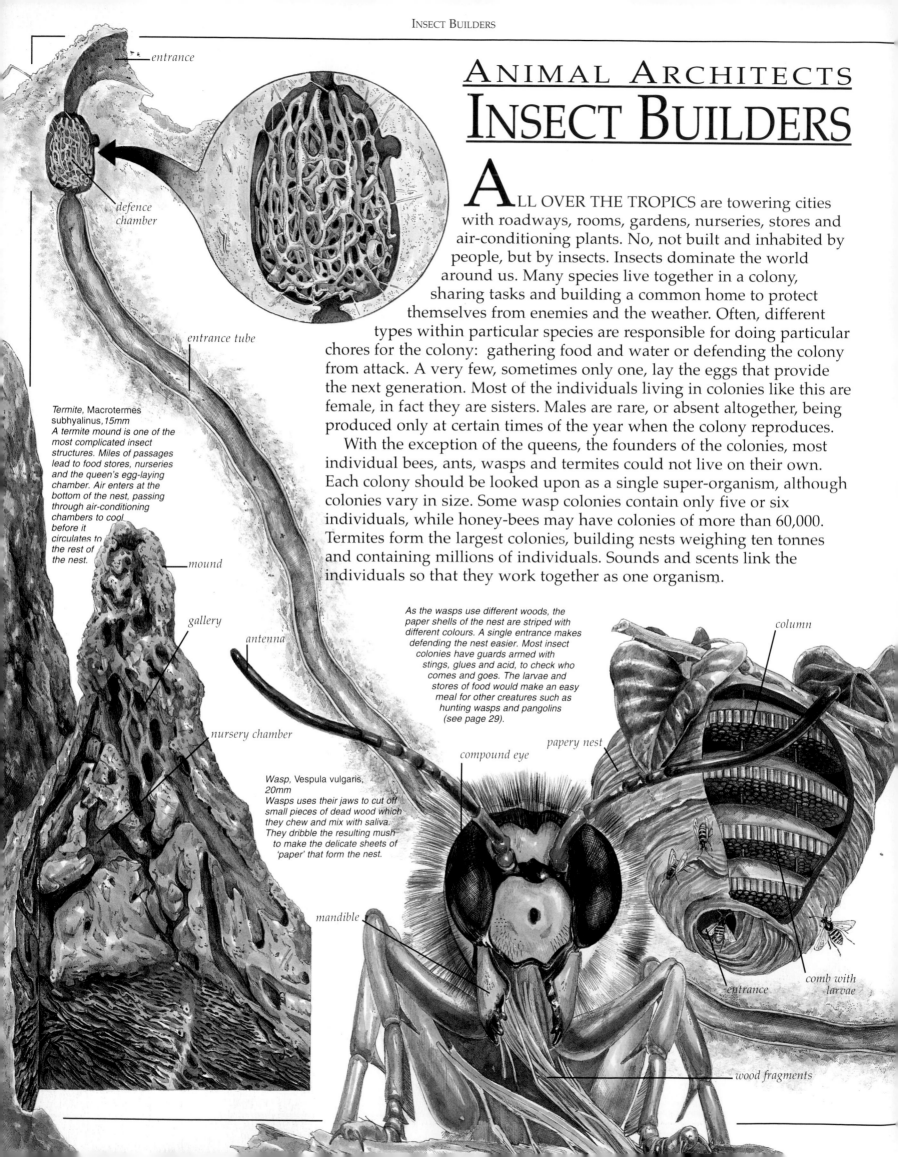

entrance

defence chamber

entrance tube

Termite, Macrotermes subhyalinus, 15mm
A termite mound is one of the most complicated insect structures. Miles of passages lead to food stores, nurseries and the queen's egg-laying chamber. Air enters at the bottom of the nest, passing through air-conditioning chambers to cool before it circulates to the rest of the nest.

mound

gallery

antenna

nursery chamber

ANIMAL ARCHITECTS
INSECT BUILDERS

ALL OVER THE TROPICS are towering cities with roadways, rooms, gardens, nurseries, stores and air-conditioning plants. No, not built and inhabited by people, but by insects. Insects dominate the world around us. Many species live together in a colony, sharing tasks and building a common home to protect themselves from enemies and the weather. Often, different types within particular species are responsible for doing particular chores for the colony: gathering food and water or defending the colony from attack. A very few, sometimes only one, lay the eggs that provide the next generation. Most of the individuals living in colonies like this are female, in fact they are sisters. Males are rare, or absent altogether, being produced only at certain times of the year when the colony reproduces.

With the exception of the queens, the founders of the colonies, most individual bees, ants, wasps and termites could not live on their own. Each colony should be looked upon as a single super-organism, although colonies vary in size. Some wasp colonies contain only five or six individuals, while honey-bees may have colonies of more than 60,000. Termites form the largest colonies, building nests weighing ten tonnes and containing millions of individuals. Sounds and scents link the individuals so that they work together as one organism.

As the wasps use different woods, the paper shells of the nest are striped with different colours. A single entrance makes defending the nest easier. Most insect colonies have guards armed with stings, glues and acid, to check who comes and goes. The larvae and stores of food would make an easy meal for other creatures such as hunting wasps and pangolins (see page 29).

column

papery nest

compound eye

Wasp, Vespula vulgaris, 20mm
Wasps uses their jaws to cut off small pieces of dead wood which they chew and mix with saliva. They dribble the resulting mush to make the delicate sheets of 'paper' that form the nest.

mandible

entrance

comb with larvae

wood fragments

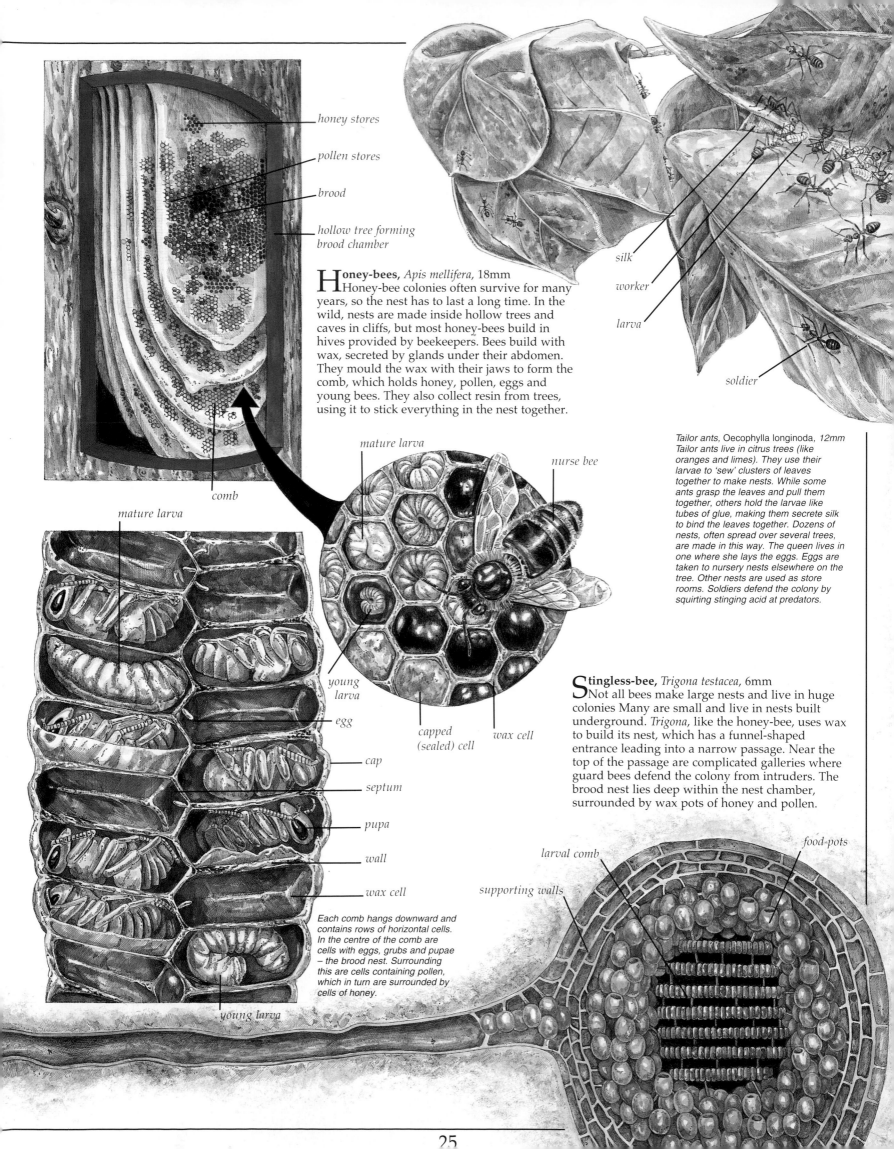

honey stores

pollen stores

brood

hollow tree forming
brood chamber

comb

silk

worker

larva

soldier

Honey-bees, *Apis mellifera*, 18mm
Honey-bee colonies often survive for many
years, so the nest has to last a long time. In the
wild, nests are made inside hollow trees and
caves in cliffs, but most honey-bees build in
hives provided by beekeepers. Bees build with
wax, secreted by glands under their abdomen.
They mould the wax with their jaws to form the
comb, which holds honey, pollen, eggs and
young bees. They also collect resin from trees,
using it to stick everything in the nest together.

mature larva

nurse bee

mature larva

young
larva

egg

cap

septum

pupa

wall

wax cell

capped
(sealed) cell

wax cell

Tailor ants, Oecophylla longinoda, *12mm*
Tailor ants live in citrus trees (like
oranges and limes). They use their
larvae to 'sew' clusters of leaves
together to make nests. While some
ants grasp the leaves and pull them
together, others hold the larvae like
tubes of glue, making them secrete silk
to bind the leaves together. Dozens of
nests, often spread over several trees,
are made in this way. The queen lives in
one where she lays the eggs. Eggs are
taken to nursery nests elsewhere on the
tree. Other nests are used as store
rooms. Soldiers defend the colony by
squirting stinging acid at predators.

Stingless-bee, *Trigona testacea*, 6mm
Not all bees make large nests and live in huge
colonies Many are small and live in nests built
underground. *Trigona*, like the honey-bee, uses wax
to build its nest, which has a funnel-shaped
entrance leading into a narrow passage. Near the
top of the passage are complicated galleries where
guard bees defend the colony from intruders. The
brood nest lies deep within the nest chamber,
surrounded by wax pots of honey and pollen.

Each comb hangs downward and
contains rows of horizontal cells.
In the centre of the comb are
cells with eggs, grubs and pupae
– the brood nest. Surrounding
this are cells containing pollen,
which in turn are surrounded by
cells of honey.

young larva

larval comb

supporting walls

food-pots

eye

nostril

trachea

oesophagus

upper arm bone

muscle

lung

rib

claw

stomach

Three-toed sloth, *Bradypus tridactylus*, head to tail 65cm
Sloths live in the forests of South America. They spend most of their time high up in trees, slowly and quietly eating leaves. These slow-moving herbivores might seem an easy prey for jaguars and other predators, but they are well camouflaged. Their long fur is a living community of insects, mites and algae. The algae colours the fur green, camouflaging the sloth. Once a week sloths descend to the ground to defecate. Moths which live in their fur jump off and lay their eggs in the dung. The eggs hatch and the caterpillars feed on the nutritious dung. They later pupate, emerging as adult moths which fly up into the trees to find another sloth.

INCREDIBLE WAYS
CLEVER CAMOUFLAGE

EVERY CREATURE has to solve the problems of finding food, reproducing successfully and avoiding being eaten by others. No single creature exists on its own, each one is part of a community. It has evolved with other animals, plants and the physical world around it (climate, weather, rocks and soil). The organisms making up a community interact and depend upon one another. Communities can range from the fur coat of a mammal, with its skin, hair, lice, fleas, mites and even algae, to a coral reef, with its different corals, fish, worms, sea urchins, shrimps and sponges.

An animal's shape, size, colour and habits reflects its success and fitness to survive, find food, avoid being eaten, find a mate and so ensure its species' survival. Unsuccessful creatures die before they can reproduce, only the fittest survive. Survival techniques take different forms. Not everything is what it may seem! A 'twig' or a 'leaf' suddenly walks. Some 'tree bark' flies. A 'stone' swims. Harmless plant-eating creatures try not to be eaten and hunters must not be seen by their prey.

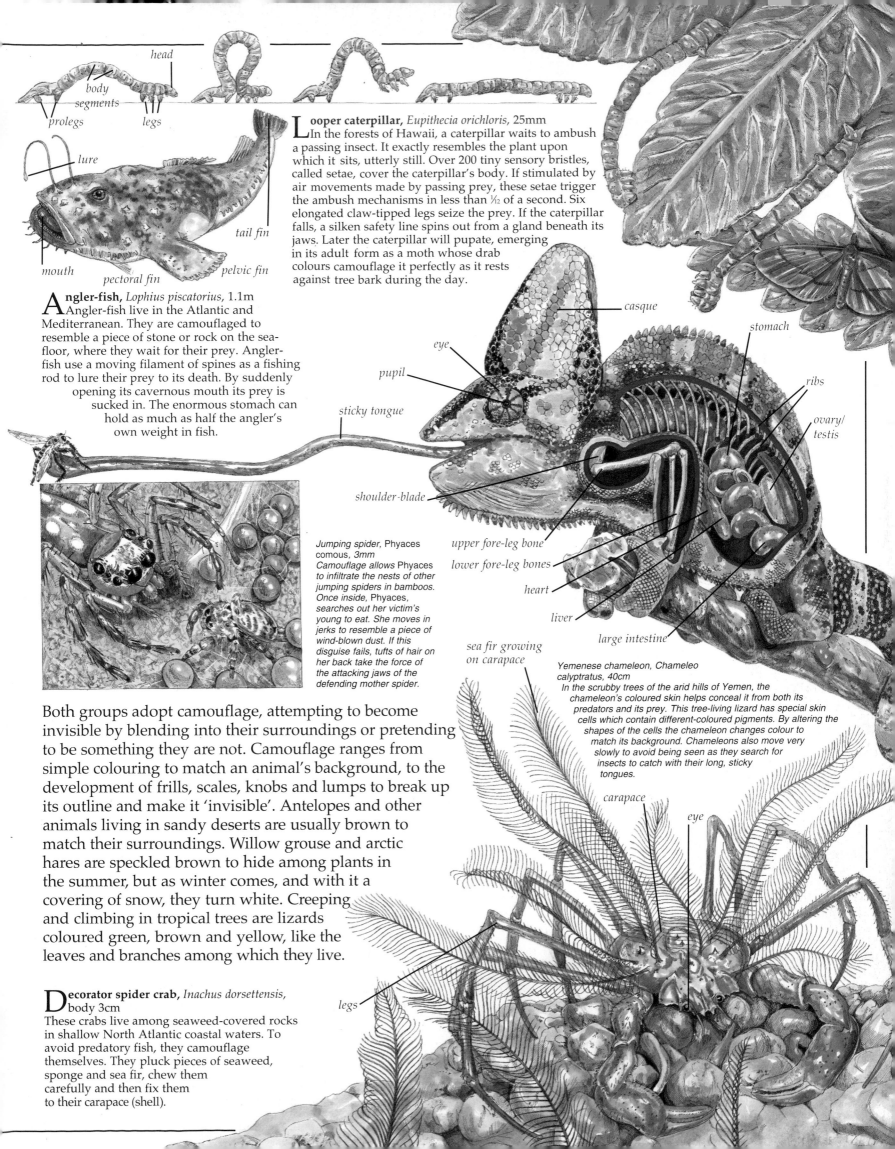

head
body segments
legs
prolegs
lure
mouth
pectoral fin
pelvic fin
tail fin

Looper caterpillar, *Eupithecia orichloris*, 25mm
In the forests of Hawaii, a caterpillar waits to ambush a passing insect. It exactly resembles the plant upon which it sits, utterly still. Over 200 tiny sensory bristles, called setae, cover the caterpillar's body. If stimulated by air movements made by passing prey, these setae trigger the ambush mechanisms in less than ½ of a second. Six elongated claw-tipped legs seize the prey. If the caterpillar falls, a silken safety line spins out from a gland beneath its jaws. Later the caterpillar will pupate, emerging in its adult form as a moth whose drab colours camouflage it perfectly as it rests against tree bark during the day.

Angler-fish, *Lophius piscatorius*, 1.1m
Angler-fish live in the Atlantic and Mediterranean. They are camouflaged to resemble a piece of stone or rock on the sea-floor, where they wait for their prey. Angler-fish use a moving filament of spines as a fishing rod to lure their prey to its death. By suddenly opening its cavernous mouth its prey is sucked in. The enormous stomach can hold as much as half the angler's own weight in fish.

casque
stomach
eye
pupil
ribs
ovary/ testis
sticky tongue
shoulder-blade
upper fore-leg bone
lower fore-leg bones
heart
liver
large intestine

Jumping spider, Phyaces comous, 3mm
Camouflage allows Phyaces to infiltrate the nests of other jumping spiders in bamboos. Once inside, Phyaces, searches out her victim's young to eat. She moves in jerks to resemble a piece of wind-blown dust. If this disguise fails, tufts of hair on her back take the force of the attacking jaws of the defending mother spider.

sea fir growing on carapace

Yemenese chameleon, Chameleo calyptratus, 40cm
In the scrubby trees of the arid hills of Yemen, the chameleon's coloured skin helps conceal it from both its predators and its prey. This tree-living lizard has special skin cells which contain different-coloured pigments. By altering the shapes of the cells the chameleon changes colour to match its background. Chameleons also move very slowly to avoid being seen as they search for insects to catch with their long, sticky tongues.

carapace
eye

Both groups adopt camouflage, attempting to become invisible by blending into their surroundings or pretending to be something they are not. Camouflage ranges from simple colouring to match an animal's background, to the development of frills, scales, knobs and lumps to break up its outline and make it 'invisible'. Antelopes and other animals living in sandy deserts are usually brown to match their surroundings. Willow grouse and arctic hares are speckled brown to hide among plants in the summer, but as winter comes, and with it a covering of snow, they turn white. Creeping and climbing in tropical trees are lizards coloured green, brown and yellow, like the leaves and branches among which they live.

Decorator spider crab, *Inachus dorsettensis*, body 3cm
These crabs live among seaweed-covered rocks in shallow North Atlantic coastal waters. To avoid predatory fish, they camouflage themselves. They pluck pieces of seaweed, sponge and sea fir, chew them carefully and then fix them to their carapace (shell).

legs

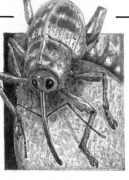

Acorn weevil, Curculio proboscideus, 14mm Weevils are beetles with long, hollow 'snouts'. Rotating its head and using tiny teeth at the tip of its

snout, the acorn weevil drills through the tough acorn shell. Females have longer snouts than males to drill a deep hole into acorns that are still on the tree. Then

they lay an egg inside the hole. When the larva hatches it eats a chamber within the acorn. Then, when the acorn falls to the ground, the larva gnaws its way out

and burrows into the soil. There it pupates, emerging the following year as an adult, ready to fly into the oak trees and repeat the life-cycle.

eye

antenna

jaw

Acacia thorn ant, Pseudomyrmex ferruginea, 10mm
Acacia plants have evolved spines as protection against grazing animals, but are defenceless against damaging insects. So they rely on ants. The ants hollow out the acacia's thorns, rearing their young there and feeding them on the tree's protein-rich leaf buds. If the tree is attacked by insects, the ants vigorously bite and sting them.

antenna

jaw

wing-cover

thorax

eye

leg

abdomen

wing

INCREDIBLE WAYS
SURVIVING TOGETHER

LIVING CREATURES HAVE FOUND incredible ways of living and feeding in almost every conceivable place. For an animal to be successful and reproduce it must find a source of food and live long enough. Plants provide food for many animals. Every part of a plant is eaten: leaves, stems, flowers, pollen, roots, tubers, wood and bark. Deer graze on grass. Caterpillars eat leaves, some even live inside the stems, leaves and roots of plants, where they are safe from predators. Plant-eaters are eaten in turn. Deer are eaten by tigers, caterpillars by birds. Instead of killing their prey, creatures like fleas, lice and some wasps are parasites and obtain their food from other living animals (hosts). Some creatures feed on dead and decaying plants and animals, so helping to 'clean-up' and recycle nutrients. This sequence of animals feeding in a community forms a complicated food web: leaf eaten by caterpillar, caterpillar eaten by lizard, lizard eaten by bird; caterpillar parasitized by wasp, wasp eaten by spider, spider eaten by bird . . . and so on.

Predators and prey, parasite and host are examples of associations between the organisms in a community. Many different and intricate associations have developed. In some cases, such as the acacia ant and the acacia plant (top left), each member of the association benefits. In others, for example parasites, one of the pair benefits at the expense of the other.

palp

termites

Pseudoscorpion, Americhernes, 4mm
Most insects have solved the problem of getting from place to place by flying. Some small, non-flying insects, mites and pseudoscorpions have evolved a different way of getting about: they hitch a lift! Pseudoscorpions cannot fly. Instead then attach themselves to a harlequin beetle. These two creatures live among rotting fig trees in South America. When female adult harlequin beetles emerge from their pupae they soon fly off in search of another rotting fig tree in which to lay their eggs. Before they do, pseudoscorpions climb on the beetles, anchoring themselves with silken threads. They climb off when the beetles land.

leg

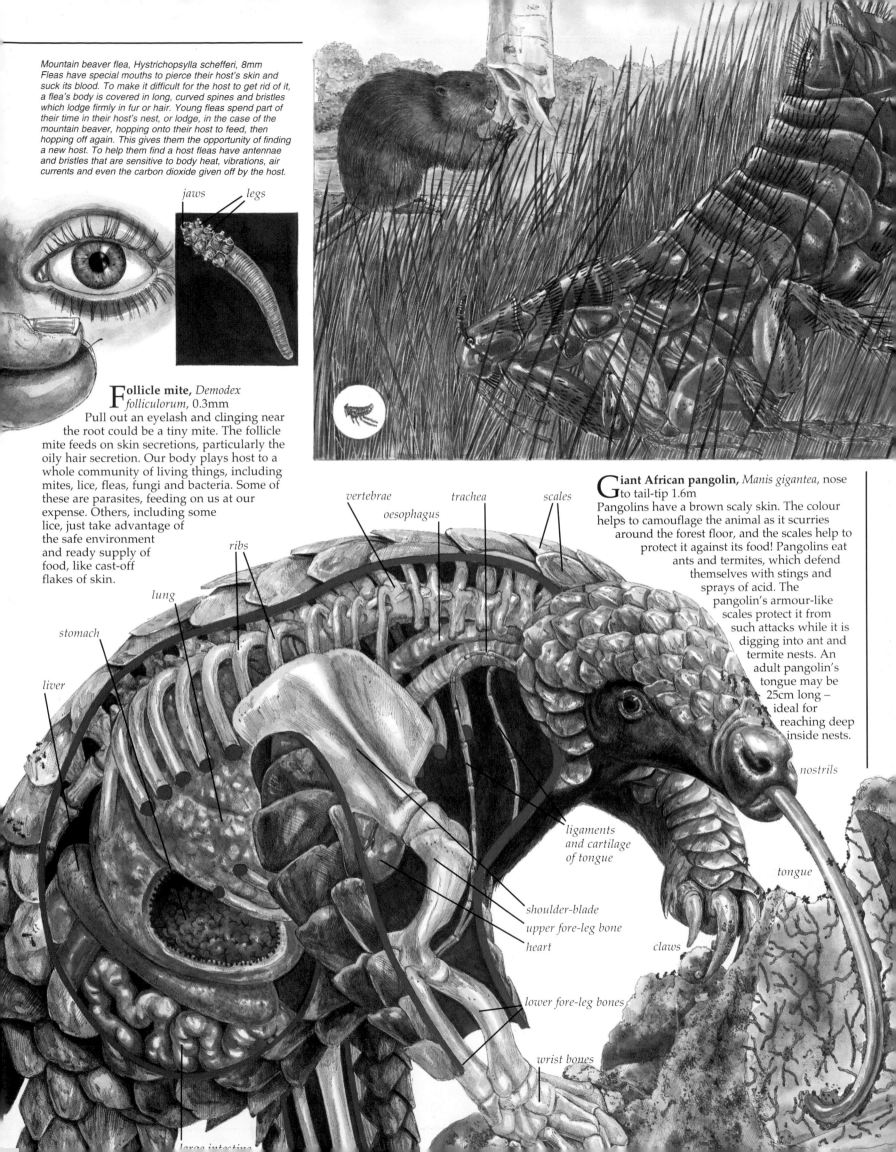

Mountain beaver flea, Hystrichopsylla schefferi, 8mm
Fleas have special mouths to pierce their host's skin and suck its blood. To make it difficult for the host to get rid of it, a flea's body is covered in long, curved spines and bristles which lodge firmly in fur or hair. Young fleas spend part of their time in their host's nest, or lodge, in the case of the mountain beaver, hopping onto their host to feed, then hopping off again. This gives them the opportunity of finding a new host. To help them find a host fleas have antennae and bristles that are sensitive to body heat, vibrations, air currents and even the carbon dioxide given off by the host.

jaws   legs

Follicle mite, *Demodex folliculorum*, 0.3mm
Pull out an eyelash and clinging near the root could be a tiny mite. The follicle mite feeds on skin secretions, particularly the oily hair secretion. Our body plays host to a whole community of living things, including mites, lice, fleas, fungi and bacteria. Some of these are parasites, feeding on us at our expense. Others, including some lice, just take advantage of the safe environment and ready supply of food, like cast-off flakes of skin.

Giant African pangolin, *Manis gigantea*, nose to tail-tip 1.6m
Pangolins have a brown scaly skin. The colour helps to camouflage the animal as it scurries around the forest floor, and the scales help to protect it against its food! Pangolins eat ants and termites, which defend themselves with stings and sprays of acid. The pangolin's armour-like scales protect it from such attacks while it is digging into ant and termite nests. An adult pangolin's tongue may be 25cm long – ideal for reaching deep inside nests.

vertebrae   trachea   scales
oesophagus
ribs
lung
stomach
liver
nostrils
ligaments and cartilage of tongue
tongue
shoulder-blade
upper fore-leg bone
heart
claws
lower fore-leg bones
wrist bones
large intestine

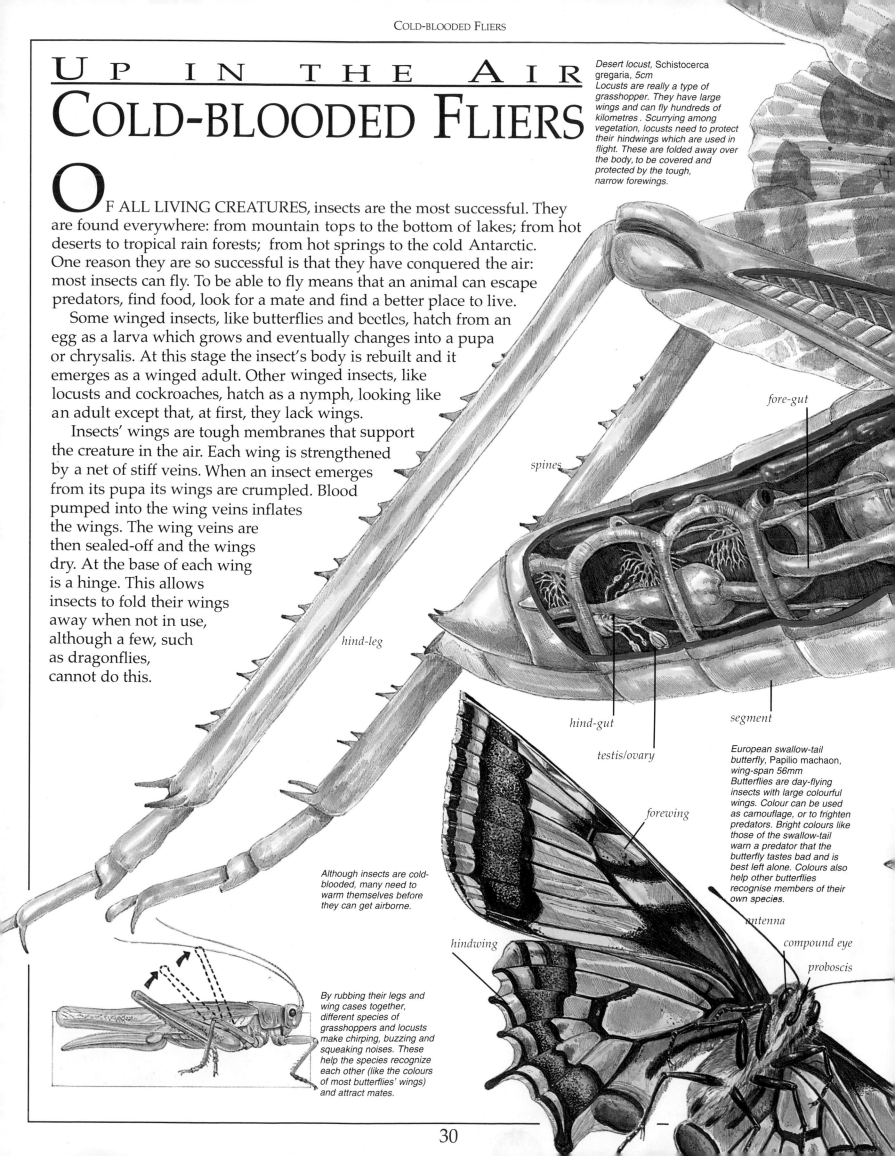

UP IN THE AIR
COLD-BLOODED FLIERS

O F ALL LIVING CREATURES, insects are the most successful. They are found everywhere: from mountain tops to the bottom of lakes; from hot deserts to tropical rain forests; from hot springs to the cold Antarctic. One reason they are so successful is that they have conquered the air: most insects can fly. To be able to fly means that an animal can escape predators, find food, look for a mate and find a better place to live.

Some winged insects, like butterflies and beetles, hatch from an egg as a larva which grows and eventually changes into a pupa or chrysalis. At this stage the insect's body is rebuilt and it emerges as a winged adult. Other winged insects, like locusts and cockroaches, hatch as a nymph, looking like an adult except that, at first, they lack wings.

Insects' wings are tough membranes that support the creature in the air. Each wing is strengthened by a net of stiff veins. When an insect emerges from its pupa its wings are crumpled. Blood pumped into the wing veins inflates the wings. The wing veins are then sealed-off and the wings dry. At the base of each wing is a hinge. This allows insects to fold their wings away when not in use, although a few, such as dragonflies, cannot do this.

Desert locust, Schistocerca gregaria, 5cm
Locusts are really a type of grasshopper. They have large wings and can fly hundreds of kilometres . Scurrying among vegetation, locusts need to protect their hindwings which are used in flight. These are folded away over the body, to be covered and protected by the tough, narrow forewings.

fore-gut

spines

hind-leg

hind-gut

testis/ovary

segment

European swallow-tail butterfly, Papilio machaon, wing-span 56mm
Butterflies are day-flying insects with large colourful wings. Colour can be used as camouflage, or to frighten predators. Bright colours like those of the swallow-tail warn a predator that the butterfly tastes bad and is best left alone. Colours also help other butterflies recognise members of their own species.

forewing

Although insects are cold-blooded, many need to warm themselves before they can get airborne.

hindwing

antenna

compound eye

proboscis

By rubbing their legs and wing cases together, different species of grasshoppers and locusts make chirping, buzzing and squeaking noises. These help the species recognize each other (like the colours of most butterflies' wings) and attract mates.

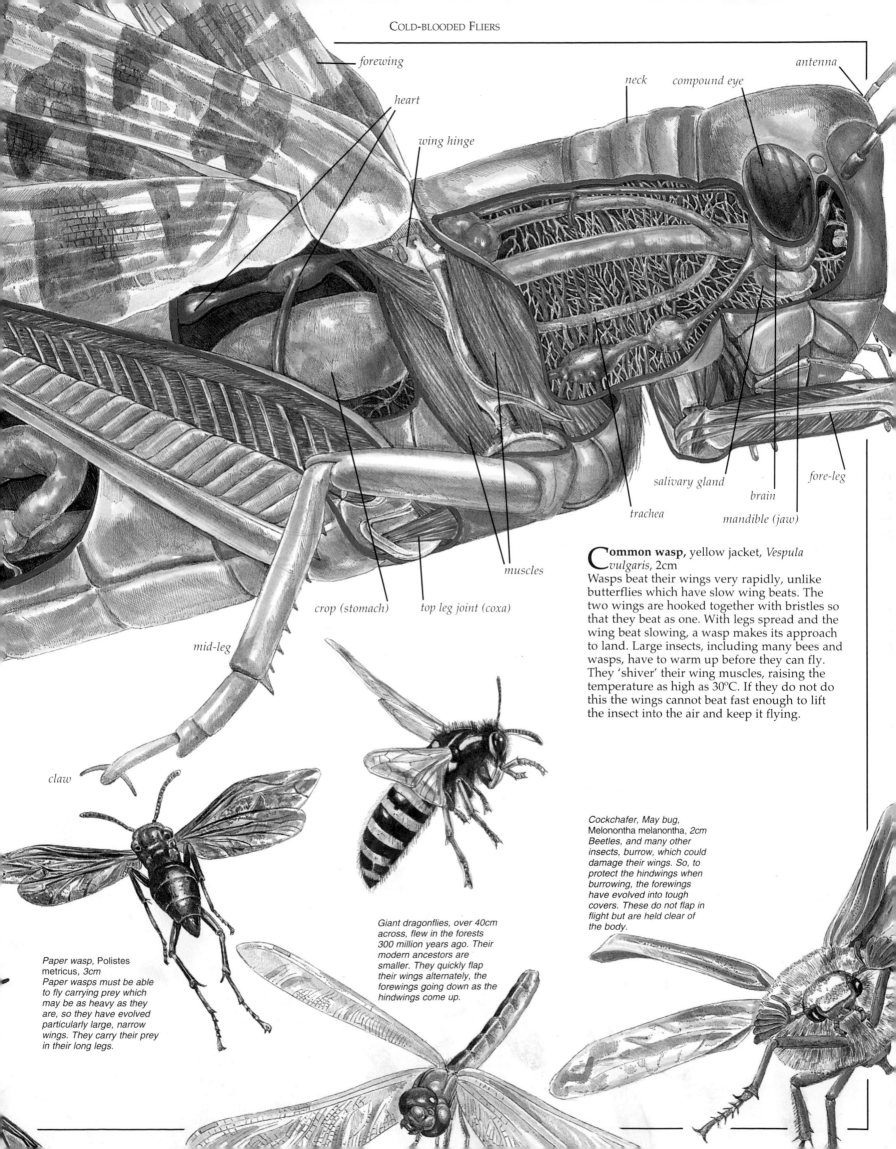

forewing

heart

wing hinge

neck

compound eye

antenna

muscles

crop (stomach)

top leg joint (coxa)

mid-leg

claw

trachea

salivary gland

brain

mandible (jaw)

fore-leg

Common wasp, yellow jacket, *Vespula vulgaris*, 2cm
Wasps beat their wings very rapidly, unlike butterflies which have slow wing beats. The two wings are hooked together with bristles so that they beat as one. With legs spread and the wing beat slowing, a wasp makes its approach to land. Large insects, including many bees and wasps, have to warm up before they can fly. They 'shiver' their wing muscles, raising the temperature as high as 30°C. If they do not do this the wings cannot beat fast enough to lift the insect into the air and keep it flying.

Cockchafer, May bug, Melonontha melanontha, 2cm
Beetles, and many other insects, burrow, which could damage their wings. So, to protect the hindwings when burrowing, the forewings have evolved into tough covers. These do not flap in flight but are held clear of the body.

Giant dragonflies, over 40cm across, flew in the forests 300 million years ago. Their modern ancestors are smaller. They quickly flap their wings alternately, the forewings going down as the hindwings come up.

Paper wasp, Polistes metricus, 3cm
Paper wasps must be able to fly carrying prey which may be as heavy as they are, so they have evolved particularly large, narrow wings. They carry their prey in their long legs.

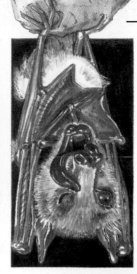

Birds and bats are warm-blooded, unlike lizards, frogs and insects which are cold-blooded. Cold-blooded animals do not always have cold blood: by basking in the sun or shivering, they can warm their bodies, but they are unable to maintain a constantly warm body temperature. Cold-blooded animals are at the mercy of the climate. If it is winter or night and too cold for them to warm themselves, their body slows and they become lethargic. They cannot feed or move. Warm-blooded animals use some of their food to produce heat which keeps their body at a constant temperature. Being warm-blooded means that they can be active in cold places and at cold times, and also that their complicated brains can work efficiently.

Wawberg's epauletted bat, Epomops franqueti, wing-span 16cm
When resting, bats fold their wings against their body, rather like a blanket. Females also use their folded wings to hold their babies. Wawberg's epauletted bat lives in Africa and feeds on figs, which it eats hanging upside down by its toes.

beak

oesophagus

trachea

lung

gizzard

crop

sternum

heart

liver

stomach

intestine

leg bone

Brown pelican, Pelecanus occidentalis, wing-span 1.1m
Pelicans fly and glide above the sea, using the up draughts of air generated as the wind blows over the water. When they find a shoal of fish they land and fold their wings before swooping underwater to chase their prey.

beak-pouch

Shoebill or whale-headed stork, Africa, Balaeniceps rex, wing-span 1.2m
The strange bill of this stork is ideal for catching frogs, fish and snakes and carrying water to its chicks. It has evolved large wings so it can lift and fly with these heavy loads.

Underwater, the pelican steers with folded wings, as its powerful legs and webbed feet propel it in pursuit of the fish. It catches this slippery prey in its open beak, which forms a scoop-like net. To reduce weight, excess water is drained from the beak before the pelican flies away.

Nine thousand species of birds fly with feathered wings. Humans who try to fly by copying birds fail because they are both too weak and too heavy. A special body is needed to be able to fly, with strong muscles to hold and work the wings, good eyesight and a large brain capable of dealing with the problems of flying. (Think of a helicopter hovering on a windy day or the mass of navigation aids in modern aircraft and compare them with the precision with which a tiny hummingbird hovers before a flower or migratory birds return each year to the same place!) To lighten the load, birds' skulls are thin and they have beaks instead of teeth. The bones of their bodies are hollow and filled with air. Birds' forelimbs have evolved into wings, which consist of feathers fixed to the bones of the arms. Birds, like finches, have short stubby wings which they flap quickly and in short bursts. Long-winged birds, like the condor, float on up draughts of air like a glider. Hummingbirds hover on short, narrow wings.

Fringe-lipped bat, Tachops cirrhosus, wing-span 15cm Silently swooping through a tropical forest in South America, a frog-eating bat is about to catch a red-eyed tree frog. It uses sound to detect where the frog is sitting before it picks it off the branch.

wing membrane

lung

ribs

intestines

skin

finger

Marvellous spatule-tail hummingbird, Loddigesia mirabilis, wing-span 11cm Hummingbirds have short, narrow wings which they can beat 200 times a second allowing them to hover almost in one place, or to move backwards.

UP IN THE AIR
WARM-BLOODED FLIERS

Bats are the only mammals that can really fly, although some squirrels and the 'flying' lemurs glide on membranes of skin stretched between their legs and body. Unlike a bird's wing, the wing of a bat is made of skin stretched between the body and bones of the fingers, hand and arm. Hooked thumbs help bats hold onto and clamber about the walls of caves and trees, where they rest upside down. Bats are active at dawn, dusk and during the night. Eyes are not much use in darkness and so bats use echo location to find their prey. They make very high-pitched chirps and squeaks, which we cannot hear unless using a special 'bat-detector'. These sounds bounce off things around them and the returning echoes tell the bat what is where. By this means bats can hunt and find their way in the dark. Prey is caught in the mouth and quickly transferred to a special fold of skin, like a scoop, between the back legs.

keel of sternum

primary feathers

Andean condor, Vultur gryphus, wing-span 2.1m High above the open plains, the pampas, of South America, condors search the ground for dead animals to eat. As the sun heats the ground, up draughts of warm air are produced which the condors use to soar to great heights. They also use the air that is forced up along the edges of hills and cliffs.

wing muscle

secondary feathers

pectoralis major flight muscle

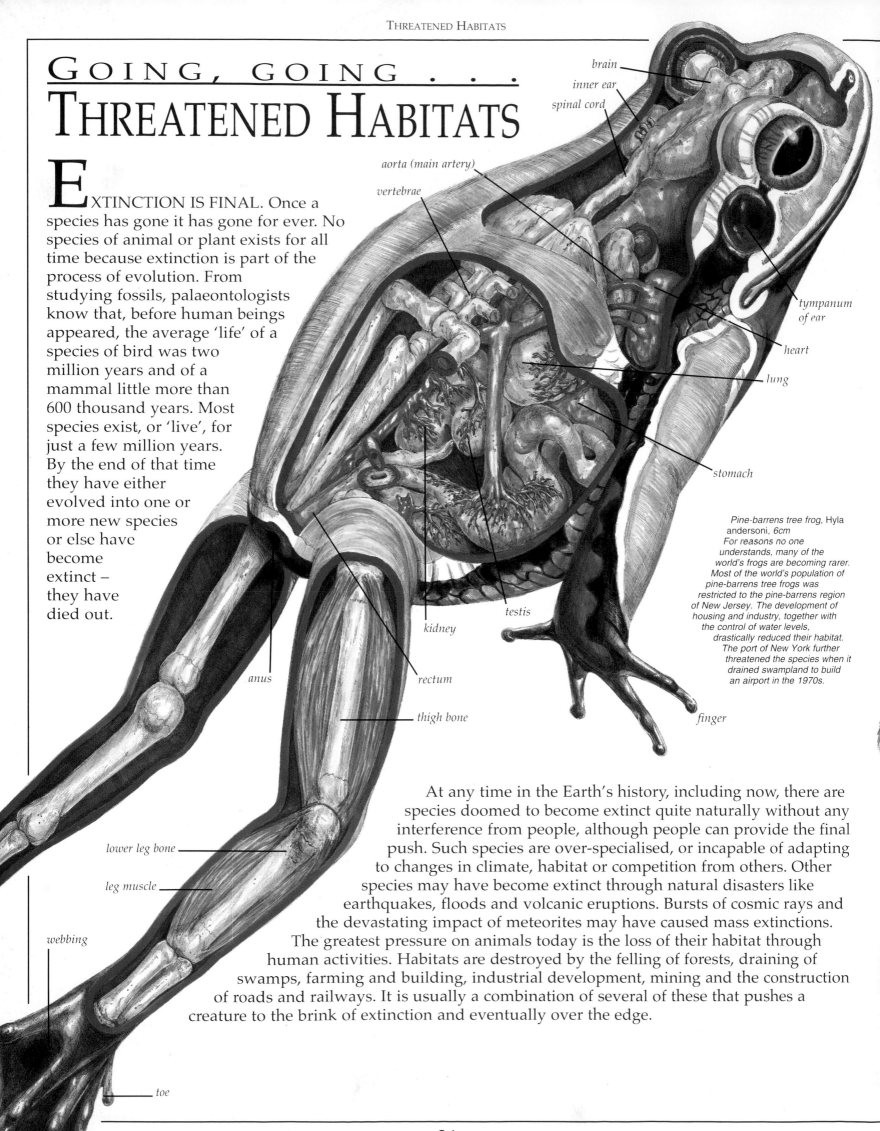

GOING, GOING . . .
THREATENED HABITATS

EXTINCTION IS FINAL. Once a species has gone it has gone for ever. No species of animal or plant exists for all time because extinction is part of the process of evolution. From studying fossils, palaeontologists know that, before human beings appeared, the average 'life' of a species of bird was two million years and of a mammal little more than 600 thousand years. Most species exist, or 'live', for just a few million years. By the end of that time they have either evolved into one or more new species or else have become extinct – they have died out.

brain

inner ear

spinal cord

aorta (main artery)

vertebrae

tympanum of ear

heart

lung

stomach

testis

kidney

rectum

anus

thigh bone

lower leg bone

leg muscle

webbing

toe

finger

Pine-barrens tree frog, Hyla andersoni, 6cm
For reasons no one understands, many of the world's frogs are becoming rarer. Most of the world's population of pine-barrens tree frogs was restricted to the pine-barrens region of New Jersey. The development of housing and industry, together with the control of water levels, drastically reduced their habitat. The port of New York further threatened the species when it drained swampland to build an airport in the 1970s.

At any time in the Earth's history, including now, there are species doomed to become extinct quite naturally without any interference from people, although people can provide the final push. Such species are over-specialised, or incapable of adapting to changes in climate, habitat or competition from others. Other species may have become extinct through natural disasters like earthquakes, floods and volcanic eruptions. Bursts of cosmic rays and the devastating impact of meteorites may have caused mass extinctions. The greatest pressure on animals today is the loss of their habitat through human activities. Habitats are destroyed by the felling of forests, draining of swamps, farming and building, industrial development, mining and the construction of roads and railways. It is usually a combination of several of these that pushes a creature to the brink of extinction and eventually over the edge.

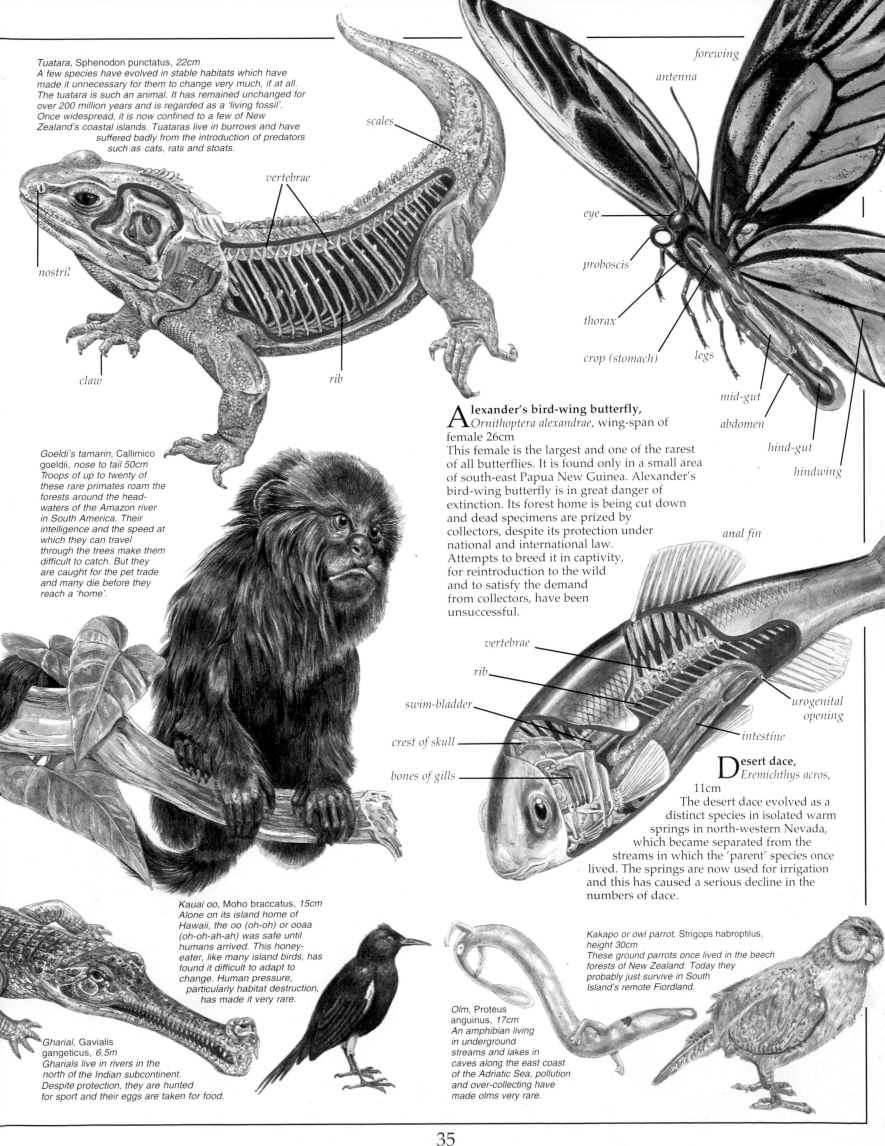

Tuatara, Sphenodon punctatus, 22cm
A few species have evolved in stable habitats which have made it unnecessary for them to change very much, if at all. The tuatara is such an animal. It has remained unchanged for over 200 million years and is regarded as a 'living fossil'. Once widespread, it is now confined to a few of New Zealand's coastal islands. Tuataras live in burrows and have suffered badly from the introduction of predators such as cats, rats and stoats.

scales

vertebrae

nostril

claw

rib

forewing

antenna

eye

proboscis

thorax

crop (stomach)

legs

mid-gut

abdomen

hind-gut

hindwing

Alexander's bird-wing butterfly, *Ornithoptera alexandrae*, wing-span of female 26cm
This female is the largest and one of the rarest of all butterflies. It is found only in a small area of south-east Papua New Guinea. Alexander's bird-wing butterfly is in great danger of extinction. Its forest home is being cut down and dead specimens are prized by collectors, despite its protection under national and international law. Attempts to breed it in captivity, for reintroduction to the wild and to satisfy the demand from collectors, have been unsuccessful.

Goeldi's tamarin, Callimico goeldii, nose to tail 50cm
Troops of up to twenty of these rare primates roam the forests around the headwaters of the Amazon river in South America. Their intelligence and the speed at which they can travel through the trees make them difficult to catch. But they are caught for the pet trade and many die before they reach a 'home'.

anal fin

vertebrae

rib

swim-bladder

crest of skull

bones of gills

urogenital opening

intestine

Desert dace, *Eremichthys acros*, 11cm
The desert dace evolved as a distinct species in isolated warm springs in north-western Nevada, which became separated from the streams in which the 'parent' species once lived. The springs are now used for irrigation and this has caused a serious decline in the numbers of dace.

Kauai oo, Moho braccatus, 15cm
Alone on its island home of Hawaii, the oo (oh-oh) or ooaa (oh-oh-ah-ah) was safe until humans arrived. This honey-eater, like many island birds, has found it difficult to adapt to change. Human pressure, particularly habitat destruction, has made it very rare.

Kakapo or owl parrot, Strigops habroptilus, height 30cm
These ground parrots once lived in the beech forests of New Zealand. Today they probably just survive in South Island's remote Fiordland.

Gharial, Gavialis gangeticus, 6.5m
Gharials live in rivers in the north of the Indian subcontinent. Despite protection, they are hunted for sport and their eggs are taken for food.

Olm, Proteus anguinus, 17cm
An amphibian living in underground streams and lakes in caves along the east coast of the Adriatic Sea, pollution and over-collecting have made olms very rare.

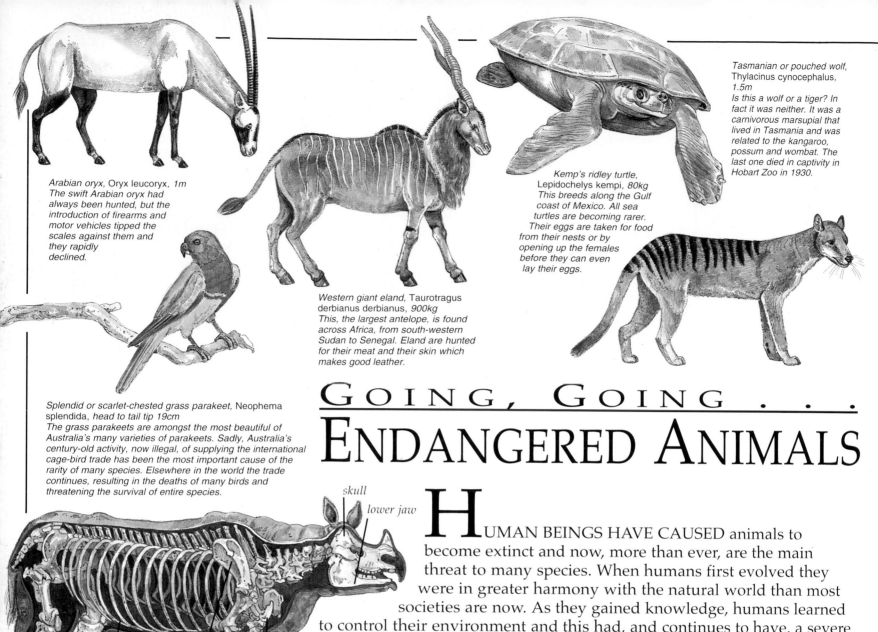

Arabian oryx, Oryx leucoryx, *1m*
The swift Arabian oryx had always been hunted, but the introduction of firearms and motor vehicles tipped the scales against them and they rapidly declined.

Splendid or scarlet-chested grass parakeet, Neophema splendida, *head to tail tip 19cm*
The grass parakeets are amongst the most beautiful of Australia's many varieties of parakeets. Sadly, Australia's century-old activity, now illegal, of supplying the international cage-bird trade has been the most important cause of the rarity of many species. Elsewhere in the world the trade continues, resulting in the deaths of many birds and threatening the survival of entire species.

Western giant eland, Taurotragus derbianus derbianus, *900kg*
This, the largest antelope, is found across Africa, from south-western Sudan to Senegal. Eland are hunted for their meat and their skin which makes good leather.

Kemp's ridley turtle, Lepidochelys kempi, *80kg*
This breeds along the Gulf coast of Mexico. All sea turtles are becoming rarer. Their eggs are taken for food from their nests or by opening up the females before they can even lay their eggs.

Tasmanian or pouched wolf, Thylacinus cynocephalus, *1.5m*
Is this a wolf or a tiger? In fact it was neither. It was a carnivorous marsupial that lived in Tasmania and was related to the kangaroo, possum and wombat. The last one died in captivity in Hobart Zoo in 1930.

skull
lower jaw
ribs   shoulder-blade   sternum
hoof
wrist

Javan rhinoceros, Rhinoceros sondaicus, *1 tonne*
Rhinoceroses are protected, but they are still killed for their horns. Rhino horn, which is really a spike made of thick matted hair, is mistakenly thought to have magical powers. On the illegal market in the Far East it is worth its weight in gold. The Javan rhinoceros has been persecuted almost to extinction, just to support the demand for horn from China.

GOING, GOING . . .
ENDANGERED ANIMALS

HUMAN BEINGS HAVE CAUSED animals to become extinct and now, more than ever, are the main threat to many species. When humans first evolved they were in greater harmony with the natural world than most societies are now. As they gained knowledge, humans learned to control their environment and this had, and continues to have, a severe effect upon animal species. Stone-age peoples caused the extinction of mammoths and many other species through over-hunting. Human hunters today kill wild animals for food, clothing, sport, status symbols, scientific study and money, and capture them for sale as pets. Humans have tried to exterminate some, like the wolf, because they are dangerous, or carry disease, or are pests and compete with people for the same resources.

trachea   shoulder-blade   liver   stomach
oesophagus   vertebrae   heart   ribs

Giant otter, Pteronura brasiliensis, *1.8m*
The giant otter of South America likes slow-running streams and rivers. In remote areas, which become smaller each year, it may still be common, but where people can reach it it is hunted and has declined catastrophically.

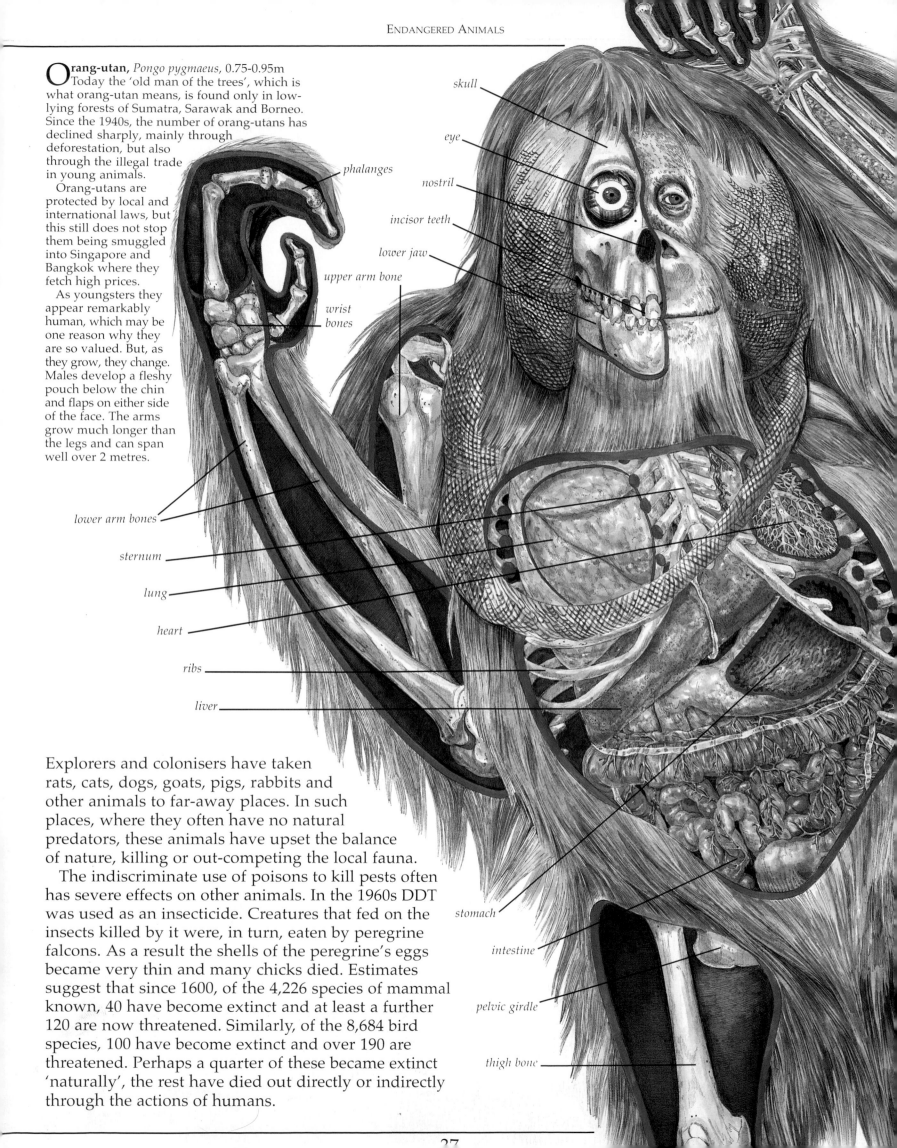

Orang-utan, *Pongo pygmaeus,* 0.75-0.95m
Today the 'old man of the trees', which is what orang-utan means, is found only in low-lying forests of Sumatra, Sarawak and Borneo. Since the 1940s, the number of orang-utans has declined sharply, mainly through deforestation, but also through the illegal trade in young animals.

Orang-utans are protected by local and international laws, but this still does not stop them being smuggled into Singapore and Bangkok where they fetch high prices.

As youngsters they appear remarkably human, which may be one reason why they are so valued. But, as they grow, they change. Males develop a fleshy pouch below the chin and flaps on either side of the face. The arms grow much longer than the legs and can span well over 2 metres.

skull

eye

nostril

incisor teeth

lower jaw

phalanges

upper arm bone

wrist bones

lower arm bones

sternum

lung

heart

ribs

liver

stomach

intestine

pelvic girdle

thigh bone

Explorers and colonisers have taken rats, cats, dogs, goats, pigs, rabbits and other animals to far-away places. In such places, where they often have no natural predators, these animals have upset the balance of nature, killing or out-competing the local fauna.

The indiscriminate use of poisons to kill pests often has severe effects on other animals. In the 1960s DDT was used as an insecticide. Creatures that fed on the insects killed by it were, in turn, eaten by peregrine falcons. As a result the shells of the peregrine's eggs became very thin and many chicks died. Estimates suggest that since 1600, of the 4,226 species of mammal known, 40 have become extinct and at least a further 120 are now threatened. Similarly, of the 8,684 bird species, 100 have become extinct and over 190 are threatened. Perhaps a quarter of these became extinct 'naturally', the rest have died out directly or indirectly through the actions of humans.

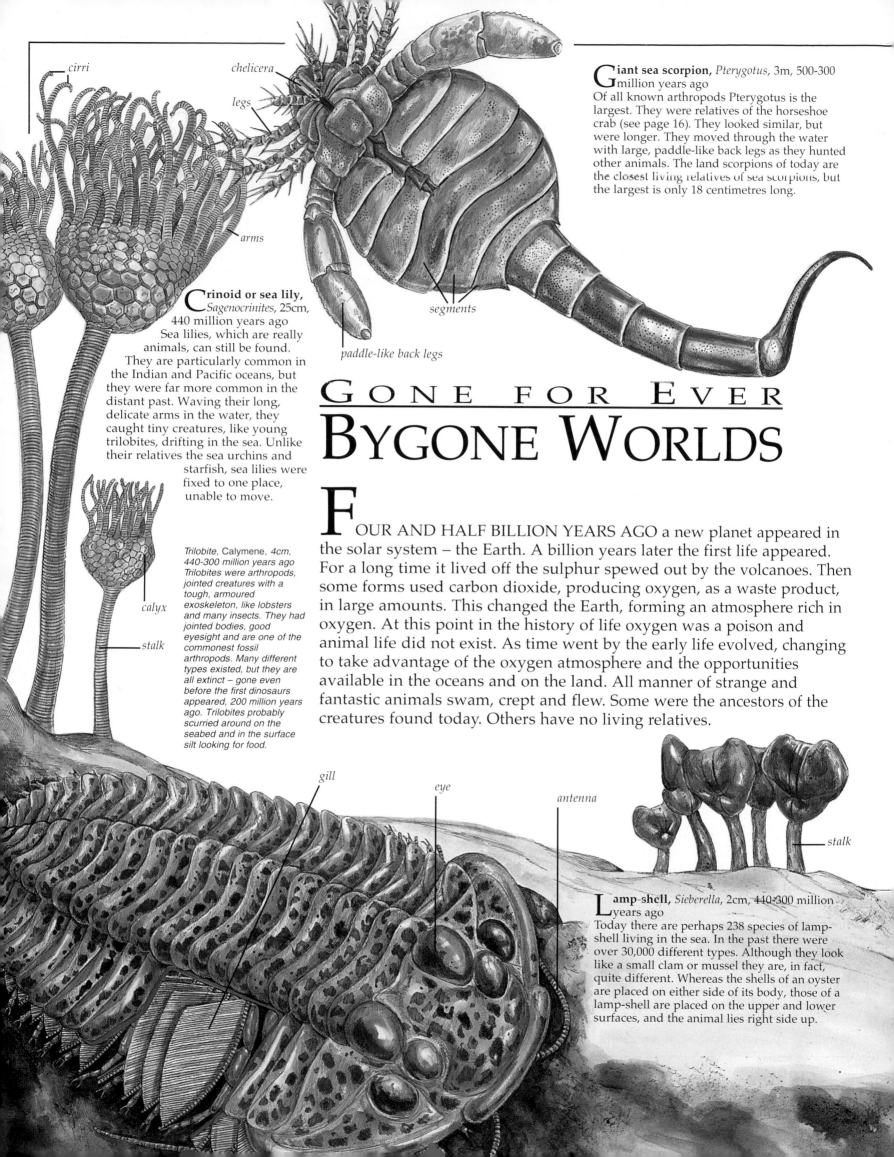

cirri

chelicera

legs

arms

Giant sea scorpion, *Pterygotus*, 3m, 500-300 million years ago

Of all known arthropods Pterygotus is the largest. They were relatives of the horseshoe crab (see page 16). They looked similar, but were longer. They moved through the water with large, paddle-like back legs as they hunted other animals. The land scorpions of today are the closest living relatives of sea scorpions, but the largest is only 18 centimetres long.

Crinoid or sea lily, *Sagenocrinites*, 25cm, 440 million years ago
Sea lilies, which are really animals, can still be found. They are particularly common in the Indian and Pacific oceans, but they were far more common in the distant past. Waving their long, delicate arms in the water, they caught tiny creatures, like young trilobites, drifting in the sea. Unlike their relatives the sea urchins and starfish, sea lilies were fixed to one place, unable to move.

segments

paddle-like back legs

Trilobite, Calymene, 4cm, 440-300 million years ago
Trilobites were arthropods, jointed creatures with a tough, armoured exoskeleton, like lobsters and many insects. They had jointed bodies, good eyesight and are one of the commonest fossil arthropods. Many different types existed, but they are all extinct – gone even before the first dinosaurs appeared, 200 million years ago. Trilobites probably scurried around on the seabed and in the surface silt looking for food.

calyx

stalk

GONE FOR EVER
BYGONE WORLDS

FOUR AND HALF BILLION YEARS AGO a new planet appeared in the solar system – the Earth. A billion years later the first life appeared. For a long time it lived off the sulphur spewed out by the volcanoes. Then some forms used carbon dioxide, producing oxygen, as a waste product, in large amounts. This changed the Earth, forming an atmosphere rich in oxygen. At this point in the history of life oxygen was a poison and animal life did not exist. As time went by the early life evolved, changing to take advantage of the oxygen atmosphere and the opportunities available in the oceans and on the land. All manner of strange and fantastic animals swam, crept and flew. Some were the ancestors of the creatures found today. Others have no living relatives.

gill

eye

antenna

stalk

Lamp-shell, *Sieberella*, 2cm, 440-300 million years ago
Today there are perhaps 238 species of lamp-shell living in the sea. In the past there were over 30,000 different types. Although they look like a small clam or mussel they are, in fact, quite different. Whereas the shells of an oyster are placed on either side of its body, those of a lamp-shell are placed on the upper and lower surfaces, and the animal lies right side up.

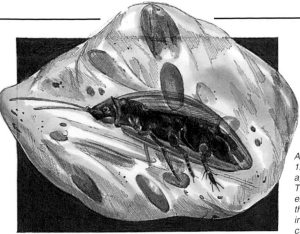

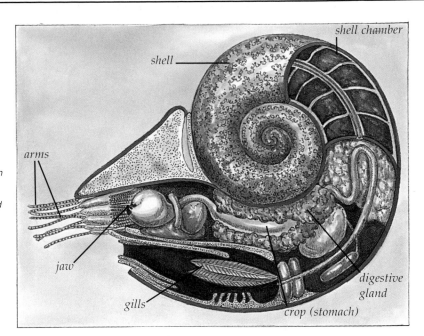

Ammonites: Phylloceras, 12 cm, 190-80 million years ago
The only cephalopod with an external shell alive today is the nautilus, the others, including squid, octopus and cuttlefish, have soft bodies. Until 135 million years ago the ammonites, another group of cephalopods with shells, were very common. They probably swam like today's nautilus, using their good eyesight for hunting and changing their depth in the water by regulating the gas inside their shell.

Amber, 160-12 million years ago
Some trees ooze sticky resin from cracks and wounds in their bark. Ancient trees also exuded resin which became fossilised as amber. Insects and other animals walking on the bark and landing on the resin millions of years ago became stuck. Many are perfectly preserved and look as if they had only just died. They closely resemble species that are alive today.

It is difficult to imagine their world, it was so different from the one we know. The Earth's surface is divided into plates beneath which the hot, semi-molten rocks of the interior are constantly on the move. These movements cause continents to move, split and join. At thin points in the surface volcanoes erupt and islands appear and later disappear. Places once tropical are now frozen. Parts of the seabed have risen and become mountain peaks. These processes take millions of years, and they are still continuing. Europe is moving away from North America at about the same speed as a fingernail grows, and India is still pushing into Eurasia and forcing the mountains of the Himalayas even higher.

Belemnite, Cylindoteuthis, 15cm, 190-70 million years ago
Belemnites were bullet-shaped cousins of the ammonites. They had an internal shell which was straight and they probably evolved from a straight-shelled ammonite, although the shell was much thicker than an ammonite's. It is from animals like this that modern squid, cuttlefish and octopus have evolved.

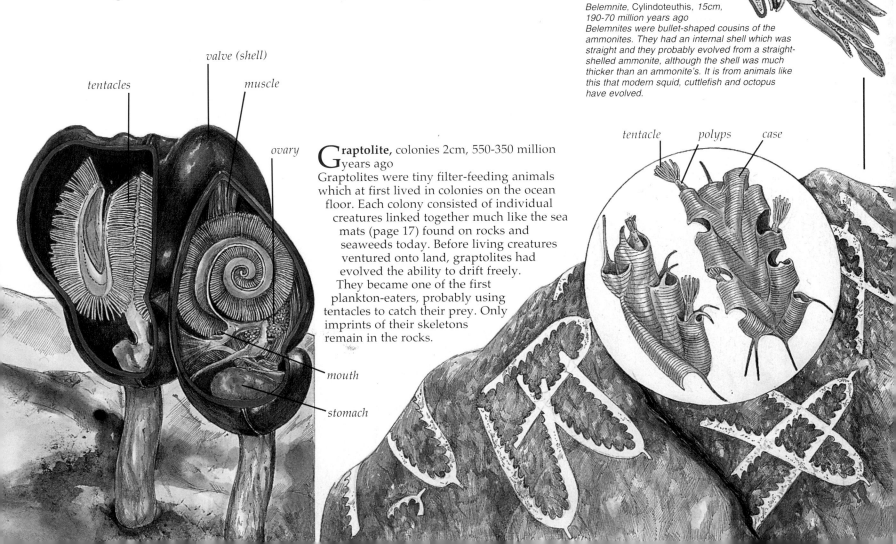

Graptolite, colonies 2cm, 550-350 million years ago
Graptolites were tiny filter-feeding animals which at first lived in colonies on the ocean floor. Each colony consisted of individual creatures linked together much like the sea mats (page 17) found on rocks and seaweeds today. Before living creatures ventured onto land, graptolites had evolved the ability to drift freely. They became one of the first plankton-eaters, probably using tentacles to catch their prey. Only imprints of their skeletons remain in the rocks.

Pakisetus, 2.2m, 58 million years ago
Pakisetus is the earliest known ancestor of modern whales, porpoises and dolphins. It swam in the ancient Tethys Sea where India, Pakistan and the Middle East are today. Like present-day sea lions, Pakisetus was not completely aquatic and probably ventured on to land to breed, using its flipper-like forelegs to pull itself along.

Gone for Ever
Fossils in the Rocks

FOSSILS, WHICH ARE TRACES of an extinct animal or plant, are usually the only clues to the life that once inhabited the Earth. A tiger kills an antelope. Vultures strip the remains, then beetles, the sun and rain reduce the carcass to bones. With luck, these become buried and over time change to become fossils. The chance of this happening is extremely rare. Rivers and floods carrying sediment to cover the remains are the most important factors in the formation of fossils. Sea creatures die and fall to the seabed where they are eaten. But there might be some remains: teeth, bones, entire skeletons or just an impression of the body in the soft silt. These remains become buried, squashed and fossilised when the sediment is compressed into rock. Mammals living away from water are less likely to be fossilised than those living near it, but all visit water at some time to drink. Others die in caves where their remains are undisturbed. In North America a few have fallen into tar pits and have been almost completely preserved. Not all extinct creatures are ancient and known only from their fossils. The dodo and passenger pigeon were exterminated by man within the last 400 years. The North American bison almost suffered the same fate, but the species has recovered thanks to breeding in zoos.

Passenger pigeon, Ectopistes migratorius, 24cm
Huge flocks of passenger pigeons moved across forested North America searching for acorns and nuts to eat.

The largest flocks of passenger pigeons blackened the skies. One flock was estimated to consist of over two billion birds! By 1900, settlers had shot the last wild bird. In one 'shoot' a billion were killed. 'Martha', the last passenger pigeon, died in Cincinnati Zoo in 1914.

Dodo, Raphus cucullatus, 1m tall, extinct 17th century
Dodos were giant, flightless pigeons, weighing between 10.6 and 17.5kg. They had feet with three toes forward and one toe behind, tiny wings and a large head with a hooked beak and bald face. They ate plants, seeds and fruits.

Dodos were ground-living birds on Mauritius, where they had no predators. However, people introduced pigs, dogs, rats and cats which found the eggs, young and adult birds easy prey. The dodo also provided easy food for sailors travelling the Indian Ocean. Discovered in the 15th century, the dodo was extinct by the 17th century.

nostril
upper jaw
oesophagus
pharynx
vertebrae
crop
tertiary feathers
secondary feathers
primary feathers
furcula (wish-bone)
sternum (breastbone)
oviduct
intestines
heart
shin bone
lung

Desmostylus, *sea horse,
1.75m, 24 million years ago*
Desmostylus *lived in the
coastal waters of the
northern Pacific, feeding
like a walrus on
molluscs, or perhaps
like a hippopotamus
on plants.*

Giant deer or Irish elk,
Megaloceros, *antler span
3.7m, 1.9 million years ago*
*This was the largest deer
roaming the woodlands that
stretched from China to
Ireland two million years
ago. The stags had huge
antlers, and the older the
stag the larger the antlers.
Fossil antlers have marks
where the stags locked
them together, pushing their
opponent to and fro just as
they do today.*

Dimetrodon, *3m, 285 million
years ago*
*Ancestors of today's
mammals, the 'mammal-like-
reptiles' lived 300 million
years ago, long before the
dinosaurs. To become
active, cold-blooded reptiles
usually warm themselves in
the sun; to cool off, they
seek shade. Dimetrodon's
sail helped in this
warming and cooling
process.*

*The sail was quite thin and
had many blood vessels.
This enabled Dimetrodon to
warm up rapidly each
morning, giving it an
advantage over more
sluggish species. If it was
too hot it could stand in the
shade and the blood in the
sail quickly cooled down.*

nostril

canine teeth

eye

ear

tongue

molar teeth

shoulder muscle

chest muscle

stomach muscle

leg muscles

A**ndrewsarchus**, 2.8m (without the tail), 35 million
years ago
Andrewsarchus must have been a frightening creature as it
roamed the plains of Mongolia. It was gigantic, with a
skull that was over a metre long. Its five toes ended in
small, sharp, hoof-like structures. It probably lived in
much the same way as today's hyenas, hunting, but more
often scavenging for food, chasing away predators, such
as ancestors of the big cats (lions and tigers), and
stealing their kill. Despite its habits, *Andrewsarchus*
was not a member of the Carnivora, the group to
which the cats, bears, and dogs belong. It belonged
to a group of mammals that included some that
were plant-eaters. Some of *Andrewsarchus*'s
relatives eventually gave rise to the whales.

Struggles between good and evil are found in many dragon myths. The Egyptians had a serpent-dragon called Apep, who daily threatened to engulf Ra, the sun god. At night Seth protected Ra, but during the solar eclipse Apep was successful. The Hittites who once lived in eastern Turkey had a weather god who was beaten by the dragon Illuyankas. With the help of the goddess Inaras, he eventually killed the dragon. According to St John the Divine in the Christian Bible, an angel will lock the dragon (Satan) in a bottomless pit until a thousand years have passed.

Chinese history goes back at least 4000 years, and so does the Chinese dragon. The old dragon gods later became mixed with the Budist and Hindu dragons called Nagas, the scientific name of the cobra. Many nagas lived in fabulous underwater palaces, had magical powers and carried large pearls in their foreheads. Chinese dragons usually laid their eggs on hillsides near water, and it rained and thundered when the eggs hatched. Each dragon always had four legs and eighty-one scales: nine times nine. The number nine had a special significance, representing Yang, one of the interlocking principles of the Universe, and meant heaven, light, vigour and masculinity. Imperial dragons were special and different from the common kinds, having five claws instead of only three or four.

The Babylonian god, Apsu, who was male, was the spirit of fresh water and of the void in which the world existed, while Tiamat was a dragon and female, the spirit of salt-water and chaos. She was fearsome, ever-changing and chaotic like her offspring. Dragons often symbolised evil, chaos and violent natural forces.

MYTHICAL MONSTERS
DRAGONS

SINCE TIME BEGAN, dragons have been both feared and regarded with wonder. In Europe, Greece and China they were familiar creatures that everyone knew about and were accepted as part of everyday life. Even four hundred years ago there were as many sightings of dragons as there were of whales. Many stories about the Earth's creation have dragons playing important roles. The Babylonian Creation Epic involves male and female forms, Apsu and Tiamat, who produced many gods, all of whom were troublesome. Apsu was tired of his children's misbehaviour and planned to destroy them. Unfortunately they heard of this and murdered him. Tiamat was furious and produced an army of fearsome gods to avenge the death of her husband. But Marduk, one of her earlier offspring and the god of storms, used lightning to kill her. He also slew her army of gods. By killing his mother, Marduk became ruler of the universe. He made heaven and earth, and, using the blood of one of the slain gods, 'Man'.

Dragons have featured as symbols of wisdom and good fortune, as well as evil, appearing on the battle standards of the Romans and Vikings. Chinese emperors used them as their imperial symbol and one still appears on the Welsh flag. Many civilisations regard certain powerful and strange wild creatures with fear, reverence and awe, and snakes and crocodiles could well have given rise to dragon myths. By the mid-17th century the existence of dragons began to be doubted. Despite this, 'dragons' were still exhibited. In 1734 a seven-headed hydra was displayed in Hamburg. But it was a fake made from parts of several different animals.

Many-headed and single-headed dragons appear throughout Jewish and Christian history, centring on Leviathan. A detailed account of Leviathan is given in the Book of Job, where he is described as having a single head, a body covered in impenetrable scales, a burning gaze and fiery breath. This dragon was the 'ancestor' of later dragons. These dragons represented evil and chaos which only goodness, faith, prayer and divine help could overcome. The word 'typhoon' comes from the Greeks, whose gods included a monstrous dragon called Typhon. Using thunderbolts the god Zeus beat Typhon and then imprisoned him under the volcano Mount Etna.

hieroglyph for Bennu

The phoenix originated from the ancient Egyptian god Bennu, a symbol of the rising sun. Like the sun rising above the horizon, the phoenix was born from its own ashes. Only one was alive at a time. After 500 years it built a nest of spices and died. Then it was consumed in a fire. From the ashes came forth a new, young phoenix.

The griffin had a lion's body and an eagle's head. The Greeks and Romans believed that it inhabited Scythia, an area that included the steppes of southern Russia, where it guarded its gold.

To the Greeks this monster was known as the basilisk, to the Hebrews as tespha (cockatrice). It was hatched by a toad from the shell-less egg of a seven-year-old cock, laid during the days of Sirius, the dog star. The basilisk was a winged beast with a dragon's tail and cockerel's head crowned with a white spot. As the king of serpents, its hiss drove away all other serpents. The breath and even a look from the basilisk were said to be fatal. Three things could kill it: a weasel, which was immune to the basilisk's deadly powers; a cock crowing; or, because it was so ugly, the sight of itself in a mirror. Today a group of lizards with an inflatable bag on top of their head and a fin-like fold down the body and part of the tail are known as basilisks.

vertebrae

skull

upper hind-leg bone

thigh muscle

comb

beak

pharynx

oesophagus

furnace

wattle

stomach

ribs

sternum (breastbone)

leg muscle

A Greek legend tells of a fabulous fire-breathing she-monster, the chimera, with a body part-lion and part-goat, and a serpent for a tail. Riding Pegasus, his winged horse, Bellerophon thrust a piece of lead into her jaws. The lead melted and poured down her throat, killing her.

MYTHICAL MONSTERS
LEGENDARY CREATURES

F ROM ALL OVER THE WORLD there are legends of fantastic and fabulous creatures. Some of these were similar to actual living animals and resulted from attempts by early explorers to explain the wonders they had`seen. In 1599 a traveller from Europe went to Constantinople (modern Istanbul) where he saw a giraffe for the first time. His description of it when he returned home made people think that it was a cross between a camel and a panther, so it was called a 'camelopard', and that is still part of its scientific name, *Giraffa camelopardalis*. For many legendary creatures there is no answer to the question of whether the creature exists or is imaginary. The International Society for Cryptozoology studies 'undiscovered' animals and searches for Loch Ness monsters and the Yeti. Every year new species of animals are discovered – so perhaps one day one of these famous monsters will be found. There is a basic human need for mystery. In the past, when science and people's understanding of the world was limited, it was easy to think that strange mythical beasts could exist. Today, as technology and science make it easier to explain the natural world, myths have changed to fit that knowledge. Unidentified flying objects, UFOs, and encounters with aliens are examples. Most will later turn out to be phenomena that were not recognized or understood. Other, new, myths will replace them.

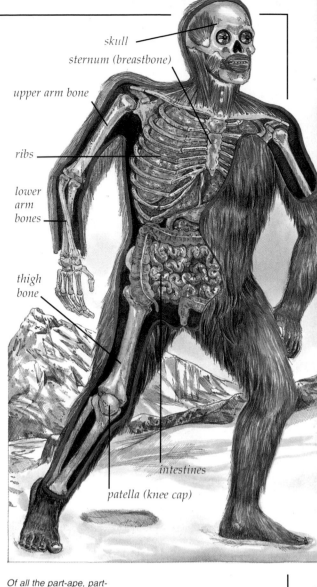

skull

sternum (breastbone)

upper arm bone

ribs

lower arm bones

thigh bone

intestines

patella (knee cap)

Nessy, the Loch Ness monster is said to live in Loch Ness in Scotland. In AD 565 Adamnan wrote about a swimmer being killed by a monster, which was commanded to leave by St Columba. For nearly 1400 years nothing more was heard of it. Since the1930s many monster sightings have been claimed. Does it exist? Nothing has been proved and a photograph, an important piece of 'evidence', has been shown to be a fake. Logs, fish, otters, and the wind on the water account for most of the sightings.

Of all the part-ape, part-human creatures said to exist, the most famous is the Himalayan Yeti or Abominable Snowman. None has ever been captured, but its footprints have been photographed.

Perhaps mermaid legends began with the ancient Akkadians of Iraq who worshipped a fish-tailed god, Oannes.

GLOSSARY

Words printed in *italics* have entries of their own.

Abdomen Rear part of the bodies of insects and *crustaceans*.

Amphibian Cold-blooded, smooth-skinned *vertebrate* which starts life as an *aquatic larva* breathing with *gills* and later undergoes *metamorphosis* to become a lung-breathing adult which can live on land.

Aquatic Living in water.

Carapace Upper body shell of tortoises and some *crustaceans*.

Carcass The dead body of an animal.

Carnivore Meat-eater.

Cell Small unit of *protoplasm* surrounded by a thin skin or *membrane*. All living things are made up of cells.

Chromosome Thread-like coiled structures in the *nucleus* of a *cell*. They carry the information needed to build the organism.

Chrysalis *Pupa* of a butterfly or moth.

Cilium/cilia Tiny hair-like structure(s) on the surface of some *cells*.

Cirri Curl-like tufts, threads or filaments.

Community Organisms that live and interact together as a group.

Continent One of the main bodies of land on the Earth's surface: Asia, Africa, Australia, Europe, North and South America and Antarctica.

Crustacean Animal with a hard outer skin, jointed limbs and two pairs of antennae.

Cytopharynx The 'gullet' or throat of a protozoan.

Cytoplasm The *protoplasm* of a *cell*, excluding the *nucleus*.

Detritus Material produced by rocks wearing away and animals and plants decomposing.

DNA Deoxyribonucleic acid; the long *molecules* which make up *chromosomes* and carry the instructions for building an organism.

Endoskeleton *Skeleton* which is entirely within an animal, for example, a bird or a human.

Energy The power of doing work.

Evolution The development (usually gradual) of new *species* from existing species through the process of *natural selection*.

Excrete To get rid of waste from the body.

Exoskeleton Rigid outer covering of the bodies of some animals, for example, insects, spiders and *crustaceans*.

Extinct No longer existing.

Extinction The process that leads to the loss, for ever, of a *species*.

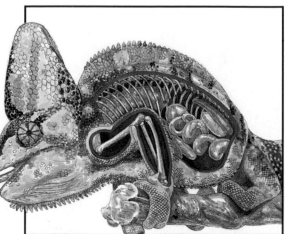

Filopodia Finger-like extensions of the bodies of some single-celled animals.

Fin Flattened limbs and ridges of tissue in *aquatic* animals, used for locomotion, balancing and turning.

Fish Cold-blooded aquatic *vertebrates* with *gills*, a streamlined body, a powerful muscular tail and, usually, paired fins.

Flagellum/flagellae Thread-like outgrowth(s) from a *cell* which, by undulating movement, can propel a small organism through water or draw particles to it.

Fossil Remains of animals and plants from bygone ages.

Gills Organs through which *aquatic* animals breathe. They take oxygen into the body and remove waste carbon dioxide.

Gnathobases Enlarged limb joints in some animals which grind together, helping crush food before it is eaten.

Habitat Place in which animals and plants live together.

Herbivore Plant-eater.

Invertebrate Animal without a backbone as part of its *skeleton*.

Larva/larvae Free-living young stage of an animal, usually distinctly different from the adult and unable to reproduce sexually.

Mammal Warm-blooded animal, usually with smooth skin covered in hair. Females produce live young which they suckle.

Marine Living in the sea.

Membrane Thin layer of *molecules* surrounding and protecting *cells*; or the thin layer of *tissue* surrounding *organs*.

Membranelle Thin flap-like projection from the surface of some single-celled animals which helps them move and also attracts food.

Metamorphosis Rapid and complete transformation from a *larva* to an adult, for example, the change from a *chrysalis* to a butterfly.

Mitochondria *Organelles* within living *cells* which convert chemicals into *energy* and allow the cells or organism to do work.

Molecule Smallest particle of a substance that can exist on its own.

Mollusc Animal belonging to a group of soft-bodied *invertebrate* animals which usually have a hard shell.

Mucous Glands which secrete *mucus*.

Mucus Slimy substance secreted by special glands and *membranes*.

Natural selection Forces that shape and maintain a *species*, including its *habitat*, the climate, and the individuals and species around it which form its community.

Nematoblast Cell containing a *nematocyst*.

Nematocyst Part of a *nematoblast* consisting of a poison sac and stinging thread.

Nucleus The part of a *cell* that contains the *chromosomes*.

Nymph Insect *larva* which hatches out looking very like the adult except that it has undeveloped reproductive organs and no wings.

Organ A combination of *tissues* which form a single structure which has one special function.

Organelle Microscopic part of a *cell* that has one special function.

Organism Living organic structure.

Osculum Large opening through which water passes out of a sponge.

Palaeontologist Scientist who studies *fossils*.

Parasite Organism which lives and feeds in or on another organism.

Phytoplankton Microscopic plants drifting and floating in the top few metres of the sea.

Plankton Animals and plants, mostly microscopic, which float and drift near the surface of the sea.

Pollution Impurities poured into the air, rivers and seas.

Polyp An animal with many feet or *tentacles*. Many of these animals are 'colonial', living together as a group. Polyp refers to individuals in the colony.

Predator Animal which hunts and preys on other, live animals.

Prey Animal which is hunted by a *predator*.

Protoplasm Semi-fluid, semi-transparent colourless substance that forms the basis of living things.

Protozoa Animals that consist of a single cell.

Pseudopodia Finger-like structures extending from the bodies of some *protozoa*.

Pupa The stage of an insect's life between the *larva* and the adult when the body is rebuilt into the adult form.

Reproduce Produce offspring.

Reproduction Act of producing offspring.

Reptile Cold-blooded, four-legged animal with scaly skin.

Resonator Hollow box-like structure which amplifies sound.

Sedentary Living fixed in one place.

Silt Very fine particles of matter drifting in water.

Siphon Tube-like structure through which water passes.

Skeleton Structure which strengthens and maintains the shape of an animal; it can also protect soft tissues.

Species Group of individuals which can breed together and produce young also capable of reproducing.

Subcontinent Large land mass forming part of a continent, for example, India.

Tentacle Slender flexible part of an *invertebrate* which is used in feeding, touching and fighting.

Terrestrial Living on land.

Tissue A combination of different cells carrying out the same function.

Vertebrate Animal with a backbone.

Zooplankton Animal life, usually microscopic, drifting and floating in the top few metres of the sea. The zooplankton, together with the *phytoplankton*, make up the majority of the *plankton* in the world's oceans.

A

Abominable Snowman 45

C

crabs 14, 16, **16**, **17**, 20
  decorator 27
  horseshoe 16, **16**, **17**, **38**
crocodiles 6, **9**, 18, 43
cytopharynx 10, **11**
cytoplasm 10, **11**, **11**, 15

INDEX

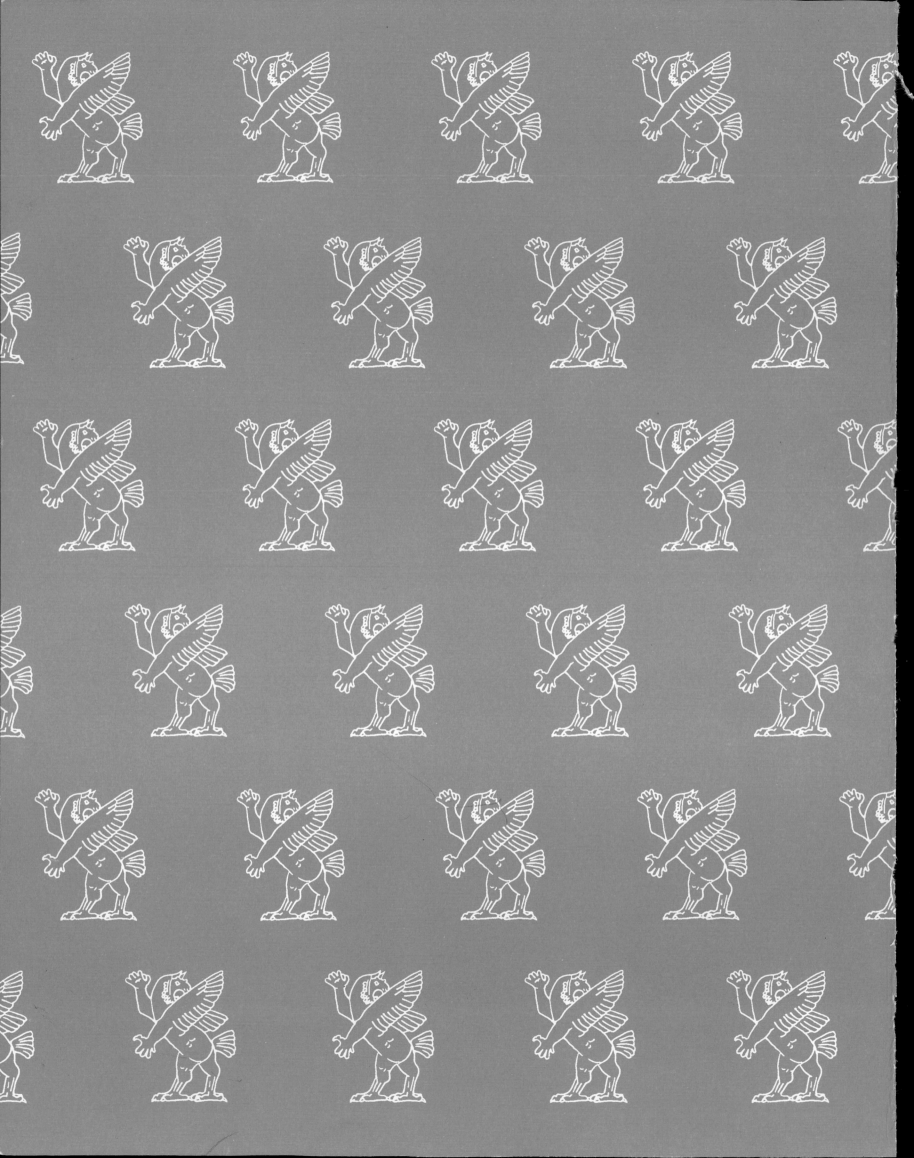